"The world is a better place be(
attitude of service to others!"

I met Al Peratt in 1989 at a 12-Step ᴋᴇᴄᴏᴠᴇʀʏ ɢʀᴏᴜᴘ.
both doing time. At that point, I had been sober for a while
and wanted to change my life. I recognized this same desire in
Al: determination to lead a new life. We soon began building
an everlasting relationship. About two-and-a-half years later,
Al was released from prison. I had no doubt then that my
new friend would make it on the outside and be successful in
whatever he chose to be or do. Our lives have taken different
paths, but Al is still a dear friend because of his faithful walk
with Christ and his choice of recovery. The world is a better
place because of Allen Peratt and his attitude of service to
others. This is such a small part of all the good things I could
say about Allen Peratt.

Reid Holiday
Commuted Lifer, Pastor Al's Mentor Within the "Walls"
Speaker on Overcoming Addiction, Maintaining Conviction

Pastor Al is a God fearing, humble man who has overcome an
extremely difficult past. This allows him to serve and mentor
many others who are battling spiritual darkness. As a man
who is full of the Holy Spirit, God has used him to advance
the kingdom and declare gospel truth to people that are lost
and broken. I have known and ministered with Pastor Al for
over 30 years. He has the heart of Jesus, full of love and com-
passion and obedient to the call of God.

Chaplain Karen Schwebach
Prison Worship Service Leader

This book, "From the Pit to the Pulpit" is going to be one of the best books you read all year. A "must hear" story from a man who has been there and done that. Pastor Al Peratt Sr. has been on the front lines as an outlaw. Now, as a person who has surrendered his life to the Lord, he is still on the front lines, only this time, he is on the winning side. You will be amazed at what a new life can look like and how dramatically a person can change and never go back to the pit. God bless you my friend, mentor, and fellow soldier in God's Army, Pastor Al.

Reverend Patrick Boll
Senior Pastor at Restoration Baptist Church
Associate Pastor at Set Free Sioux Falls
Founder and President - House of Boaz Ministry Sioux Falls

This book is well worth reading as it has been written by a man who has truly walked through the fire and now lives redeemed, restored, and set free for Christ! It's time for all of us to follow Pastor Al Peratt's example and "get busy" reaching others and serving the Lord!

Bobbi Herting
Senior Pastor SET FREE Sioux Falls
Associate Pastor Restoration Baptist Church
Executive Director of House of Boaz
(a nonprofit ministry serving women in need)
and Spiritual Advisor for inpatient addiction treatments

FROM THE PIT
TO THE
PULPIT

Pastor Allen E. Peratt, Sr.

Peratt Public Ministries

CONTENTS

Dedication

I would like to dedicate this book to a few individuals. The first is to Him who I believe saved me, Jesus Christ!

Secondly, my family. First my name family, the Peratt clan. You know who you are and some are gone from this earthly life, but never gone from my heart. Some of the best memories are of times with my brothers and sisters as we grew up. Beverly; Tom Jr.; Donald (deceased); Bill and Diane (Betty's children, both deceased). Mom's family, my second brothers and sisters: Jim (deceased), Deb, Julia, Ron (deceased), Gary (deceased), and one brother we came to know later in life. Next is my Illinois clan, the Burge's. All the many people I have come to know through my few trips back to the area where my blood Mom, Mary Jane, and my blood Dad, Earl Thomas Peratt, Sr., grew up. I concentrated on meeting my Mom's sisters, brothers, neighbors, and my next set of brothers and sisters that Mom had after divorcing my father. My grandchildren, Tanner, Deja, Dom, and Jaxyn.

Thirdly, my soulmate, wife, best friend, fellow minister of the Gospel, always-got-my-back, mother of our children, AJ, and Skylar, and just woman beyond my wildest dreams, Teresa Peratt. You know who loves you, dear, Cat-Daddy and Jesus!

I also dedicate this book to Reverend Patrick Boll, Senior Pastor, Restoration Baptist Church (previously known as Ridgecrest Baptist Church), and all my Southern Baptist brothers and sisters of the Dakota Baptist Conference, North and South Dakota.

Acknowledgements

I want all of you to know that, in each walk of my life, I have appreciated the seasonal people God put in my life. My editor, Loretta Sorensen, and her husband, Alan. Our dear friend, Nancy Loken, you have been not only a supporter, but friend of Teresa and I above and beyond. My Senior Pastor from Ridgecrest Baptist, Rev. Jesse Moore, who believed in me when I was still new from being a prodigal. The newer Senior Pastor, Patrick Boll and his Associate Pastor Bobbi Herting, who took over the reins of Set Free Sioux Falls. To Chief, Pastor Phil Aquilar, much love and respect to you for developing the original vision of Set Free OC, Orange County.

I am going to stop with names and just say I don't want to hurt anyone's feelings or "miss" someone so I say to all, thank you for your help, thoughts, and prayers throughout my life.

I will always continue to work with the "Depressed, Oppressed, Addicted and Convicted."

As my good friend JT Coughlan, a fellow Pastor from Set Free, Great Falls, Montana, says, "Stay fired up for Jesus!"

"And The Truth Will Set You Free!" John 8:32

INTRODUCTION

I waited patiently for the Lord; he turned to me and heard my cry.
He lifted me out of the slimy pit, out of the mud and mire;
He set my feet on a rock and gave me a firm place to stand.
He put a new song in my mouth, a hymn of praise to our God.
Many will see and fear the Lord and put their trust in him."
- Psalm 40:1-3

"I'm sitting in the railroad station, got a ticket for my destination . . ."

These words from the 1960's song, "Homeward Bound," clearly illustrate the thoughts I had whenever I sat in jail or prison. I asked myself, "What the hell just happened? What am I going to do now?"

My adult life has paralleled what Luke 15:11-24 describes in "The Parable of the Lost Son." I ran from God, disrespected him, and everything that I knew to be right. I squandered the opportunities and resources God provided, then blamed him for all my troubles.

I have no excuse and give no excuses for the lifestyle I chose over leading an ethical and moral way of living. In my early years, I did have a rough time. I have some dim memories of yelling, screaming, hiding under a table as two people (my parents) fought with each other. My next earliest memory is of being shuttled between different homes, "foster" homes.

At one of the homes, my brothers and I were instructed to go to our rooms because our foster family wanted to celebrate Christmas. As we hung out in our bedrooms, the three of us were acutely aware, through what we heard, that we were not welcome to take part in the celebration.

My older brother, who is much better at remembering our early life, believes we were passed between four and six homes. We finally landed with the Johnsons, a retired policeman and his wife. They were our last foster parents and were ready to adopt us. Our biological father literally had to threaten them to release us to his care again. The Johnsons hesitated to let us go because they didn't approve of Dad's new wife.

The Johnson's instincts were valid. Life with our stepmother was grueling for many reasons. However, as I approached my teen years, my parents started attending church, and I was exposed to a Christian way of living.

Those experiences helped me to some degree. However, as an adult, I spent many years wandering along a dark road, turning away from God again and again.

There was a turning point in my life in 1989, at the age of 37, when I decided it was time to change. As I've shared with others how God began working in my life, bringing me from an outlaw biker to an ordained minister, I've often been asked, "Why don't you write a book about all this?" To answer that question, here is the book.

This project has been on my "bucket" list for a long time. There are several reasons to get it written. In 2012, after being diagnosed with base-of-the-tongue cancer, I underwent 37 straight days of radiation and chemotherapy. On the 38th day, I sat in a wheelchair in my oncologist's office. Within moments of arriving, I fell out of the wheelchair and was rushed to an examining room. Doctors found that my white blood cell count was extremely low.

For the next 45 days, I was in and out of a coma. At one point, I quit breathing. Had it not been for Teresa, my wife, administering mouth-to-mouth resuscitation, I would not be alive today.

After recovering from this near-death experience, I had many high priority projects I wanted to complete before God calls me home. This account of my life is the final one.

I want to make it clear that I'm not perfect, by any means. I'm recounting my experiences to the best of my ability. Because truth is so important to me, I will not embellish nor add to my story to any degree.

Good people, I know my style of writing often has a "street" tone. Since some in my audience struggle with reading, I've tried to keep the writing style simple. I have repeated important events in some chapters to help emphasize main thoughts that may be discussed in a small group study.

By sharing my story, I hope to help another lost soul, a lost Son or Daughter, find their way out of the crazy, mixed-up world of alcohol, drugs, and crime. You may be experiencing dire times and need to find the way out of "mire and mud," to find the "solid rock" that is the only sound foundation for anyone's life. I pray my personal life journey will bring light to help you more clearly see your path for a better future.

*W*e know that the law is spiritual; but I am unspiritual, sold as a slave to sin. I do not understand what I do. For what I want to do I do not do, but what I hate I do. And if I do what I do not want to do, I agree that the law is good. As it is, it is no longer I myself who do it, but it is sin living in me. For I know that good itself does not dwell in me, that is, in my sinful nature. For I have the desire to do what is good, but I cannot carry it out. For I do not do the good I want to do, but the evil I do not want to do—this I keep on doing. Now if I do what I do not want to do, it is no longer I who do it, but it is sin living in me that does it.

So I find this law at work: Although I want to do good, evil is right there with me. For in my inner being I delight in God's law; but I see another law at work in me, waging war against the law of my mind and making me a prisoner of the law of sin at work within me. What a wretched man I am! Who will rescue me from this body that is subject to death? Thanks be to God, who delivers me through Jesus Christ our Lord!

So then, I myself in my mind am a slave to God's law, but in my sinful nature a slave to the law of sin." - Romans 7:14-25

CHAPTER ONE

THE EARLY YEARS
1948 - 1966

My two older brothers, Donald and Tom, and my sister, Beverly, grew up in El Cajon, San Diego, a suburb in sunny California!

I can't say that every day of my young life was dismal. However, much of my earliest recollections of life have been pretty dark.

Clear memories of the first three or four years of my life include intense fights between my alcoholic parents. My biological parents were high functioning alcoholics. As a member of the US Navy, Dad was also a workaholic. He was a senior non-commissioned Navy officer and a career submariner. While serving in the ship engine room, he achieved the rank of E-7, Chief Petty Officer. His Navy shipmates called him "Submarine Chief of the engine room."

Mom was a World War II riveter, working in factories where ammunition and war supplies were produced.

Due to alcoholism, their parenting skills often fell short. One clear indication of that is the long scar on the back of my neck. I'm told it was the result of my father slamming on the car brakes while we drove down the road. At the time, there were no seatbelt or child restraint laws to keep little kids like me from flying through the car's front windshield. The incident resulted in a massive gash on the back of my head. (In my gang days, to explain this major wound, I made up many lies about surviving a major gang fight.)

I was just three when my parents separated. My siblings and I began circulating through California's foster home system. My older brother Tom has often described our stay at different homes as lengthy. (Because I was so young, I don't recall those details.)

Our sister Beverly stayed with family friends in San Diego. We only saw her when Dad was home on leave.

Once we were placed in foster homes, we rarely saw Dad. Each time he came into port, our visit with him was our "Christmas!"

Dad would return in July from Okinawa with gifts such as Japanese-made jackets. Under the hot California summer sun we sported our new clothes. Year after year our neighborhood recognized our "Navy brat" status through this "Christmas" tradition.

For a significant period, my brothers and I lived with the Johnsons, a family in San Diego. Mr. Johnson was a retired cop who became acquainted with Dad through some of Dad's Navy buddies, whom he likely met in some kind of bar encounter. Dad paid the Johnsons to keep us boys. Monthly payments seemed an essential part of their agreement. There was no government oversight in this deal.

As I look back on those days with the Johnsons, it seems I was already doing time. In the dinky house where we lived, we slept in bunk beds. The backyard was my favorite hangout, although that was also where our "foster dad" raised rabbits. Every weekend Mr. Johnson was faithful to line us boys up so we could watch him catch the rabbits, beat their heads in with a hammer, and skin them. His wife fried the meat, which we found on our plates at the dinner table.

During this time, I was always getting into mischief after school. As often as possible, my brothers walked me home. Every chance I had, I hung back.

When I was with my friends, my goal was to prove myself by taking the frequent "dare" that was proposed. My desire to gain their approval regularly led me to slip into a store along the path home and shoplift some candy.

"Dare you to throw a match down that hole!" Several of us were kneeling beside what used to be a fuel tank in a now-abandoned gas station. These "friends" were older than me. In light of all the detachment I had known in my young life, it was important to me to "belong" somewhere. I dropped the match.

Suddenly, a great rumbling knocked us back from the small hole we knelt beside. As leftover gas fumes ignited, glass in the empty station building shattered all around us. No doubt about it: I was in trouble.

When the police arrived, all the other kids pointed fingers at me. The cops immediately took me home. There I dug deep within myself to come up with a convincing lie about what had happened. What could I say about how I had been an innocent bystander? That day the root of a lying habit began growing in me. This destructive pattern would follow me through many years of my life.

After appearing in court and wondering what the judge meant when he called me a "punk," part of my punishment was to scrub tires on the side of fire station trucks. Maybe that was a good thing, as the men there took me under their wing. To this day, I remember their kindness.

Between the delicious food the firemen provided, and the lectures they shared about the dangers of playing with matches, I never played with fire again.

During this period, I don't recall going to church or hearing about spiritual elements for living. I do remember I was always in trouble, and up to mischief.

The first time I ever went to church it was with some friends of the Johnsons. They stopped by the house, asking if they could pick us up and bring us to church. It was there we heard cute little stories about a guy named Jesus. My brothers and I looked forward to those church visits. Primarily because, if we were good, we went for ice cream on the way home. The concept that "Jesus Loves Me" was lost on each of us.

With all the disruption of my early life, I lacked some real basic social skills when I started going to school. Even before school started, I was hanging out with kids who were several years older than me. My first major incident was the result of getting caught shoplifting bubblegum. That didn't stop me from teaching other kids how to shoplift. My brother Donald was never good at it and my brother Tom never did get into that kind of trouble. He was more likely to do something like throwing firecrackers out the window, right under a police cruiser. Not good.

My most prominent destructive habit at that point in my life was seeing how many lies I could tell without being caught. Many times I was told that telling the truth would help me avoid a lot of trouble. My take on that advice was that I had a 50/50 chance of being believed. I chose to lie and take the beating if I was discovered.

Many years later, my siblings and I learned that we were placed in foster care because our mother had been given the wrong court date and lost all custody after she failed to appear. The lies we children heard about our mother were built up even further by a devious stepmother. Year after year, she returned letters and Christmas presents our mother mailed to us.

I suppose I could recite a litany of "Oh woe is me" stories about foster home experiences. The main point, though, is that 1950s foster homes weren't regulated.

Our lives took a new turn when Dad remarried. Betty was an East Coast schoolteacher with two children, Bill and Diane. My sister Beverly also rejoined our family.

I expected life to become much better once we had a new Mom. But we were not allowed to call her Mom. It was "Mother," "Yes, ma'am," "No, ma'am," and many other niceties that were foreign to me.

My first mistake in my relationship with Betty was to look at her closely. It was clear she wasn't my real mother. Her eyes, heavy with makeup, seemed so thin. Maybe she was Asian. At the time, post-World War II, Asians, especially Japanese, were not held in high regard in America.

Before I could stop myself, I asked, "Are you Japanese?" For years she held that childish blunder over my head.

Her response to me: "I heard you were the little liar, the black sheep of all the sons. Now I know why!"

The Johnsons added fuel to the fire by warning Betty, "Watch out for that little guy. He's quite a liar."

We weren't allowed to refer to Bill and Diane as anything other than "our brother and sister." We made no mention of step family relations.

In public, Betty could be the nicest woman. Behind closed doors, she could quickly "flip a switch" and fall into maniacal behaviors.

Despite all her shortcomings, I have to hand it to Betty. She managed to raise all six of us kids, even though Dad's Navy career took him out to sea for months at a time.

Every week we all piled into our station wagon. We went to the Navy commissary for food and other household necessities. Each of us kids had chores, and Betty was strict about keeping us and all our duties in order. She had to be entirely in charge at all times.

Despite our many conflicts, Betty's mentoring helped me in my adult life, as I learned how to cook, especially fried chicken. If it weren't for her, I wouldn't know how to set the table or understand the importance of basic manners.

On the outside, the Peratt home was one of the best-looking houses on the block. We mowed and trimmed the lawn and had attractive gardens. Every one of us kids had some kind of job: baby sitting, mowing lawns, paper routes, and both Donald and I did janitorial work at the El Cajon Chamber of Commerce. Tom bussed tables at a Country Club. Inside the house, things always had to be clean and picked up. Everything had its place. Beds were made every morning.

Part of the money we earned went into a fund to provide for our family outings. One time, when Betty decided we were too "naughty" to deserve the benefits of our pay, she took the money and bought herself some "nice things."

Over time, it became clear to us that Betty's crazed behavior wasn't reserved for her stepchildren. All of us kids were treated the same. And when Dad was home, he backed Betty up in everything she said and did.

As young as I was at that time, it seemed to me that I became Betty's scapegoat. Not that I was completely innocent. While I wasn't out stealing from anyone or breaking any laws, Betty picked up on the slightest tone of voice that might be signaling disrespect. If I looked at her wrong, the backhand or the belt would quickly come my way. The threat of that response was always in the back of my mind.

Any time Betty disciplined us boys, we were first stripped naked. Then she beat us with a belt. After repeatedly experiencing this, I began wetting the bed. Betty's response to my issue was hardly nurturing.

"I'm going to beat it out of you, boy!" she declared. I remember thinking, "What is she beating out of me?" All my life, I've carried some of the physical scars from those events.

I didn't pee the bed every night, but the nights I did, I remember how Betty pulled me out of bed and tore off the wet sheets. She herded me to the shower next to the bedroom where she and Dad slept. She pushed me in the shower, turned the cold water on, and stood guard with a broom, ready to hit me in the ribs if I tried to escape the cold shower.

I froze my butt off in those showers. The only benefit that ever came from it is my ability now to withstand a cold shower.

Looking back, I believe it was fear and ongoing nightmares that led to my bed-wetting. It's now a well-known fact that psychological turmoil can cause bed-wetting.

Betty never accepted any report card grade from any of us that was below a C. Anything less than that resulted in "restriction." That meant all homework was completed right after school, and any chores around the house were done. If you were late getting to the dinner table, your meal may or may not be served in your room. And there you were to remain for the rest of the evening. If the next report card didn't show improvement, the cycle began again.

I was so rebellious I received more restrictions than any of the other kids. Donald tried to be assertive from time to time, but Betty wouldn't allow it. Tom occasionally pushed back, but he was usually smart enough to keep still.

My sisters, Beverly and Diane, endured their share of punishment. Beverly eventually faked pregnancy so she could quickly marry and get out of the house.

One day a friend, Bill Bowen (now deceased), came to our house. He asked if I could come out and hang out with him a while. He was told that I was in trouble and wouldn't be able to have friends over for a few weeks.

Bill was genuinely puzzled about what kind of trouble would keep me restricted for several weeks. He thought I must have really messed up.

As Bill was leaving, he walked past our garage. I saw him and whispered as loud as I could through the garage door, "Bill!" He stopped and came closer to the garage door.

"Man, what's going on?" Bill asked me.

"I'm on restriction to the garage for a week. It could be for two weeks if Betty thinks I need it." I explained that my meals were delivered to the garage, and I slept there every night.

"Betty says I need to get my mind right," I told Bill. Later, Bill shared with me how he went home and told his father that he hoped he'd never be stuck in the garage for something he did. Bill's father had a hard time believing Bill's story.

Many years later, a prison psychiatrist told me he wasn't surprised that I ended up in prison after experiencing the trauma of detached foster parents and an abusive stepmother. On top of all that, I was molested by my father's best friend. But that's another story.

Today I know that it would have been okay for me to tell someone what was happening to me, how Betty was treating me. I would have been able to get help instead of living in fear.

It's excruciating to relate all these childhood experiences because I have great respect for my father, mother, and stepmother. I couldn't share any of this while any of them were still alive. I'm thankful that all my siblings believe in the value of sharing our experiences.

Believe it or not, one of the good things my stepmother did was start taking us kids to church, a Baptist church. Although it really burned me that she'd put on such a show for everyone there, then turn on us kids like a madwoman at home, I found some peace when I was in church.

I got involved in the youth group and even became a member of the church choir. I should have known this little slice of tranquility wouldn't last.

I was 14 when I landed in trouble for not attending a Youth for Christ meeting. Instead, I went to a high school dance the local police put on. My infraction led to a required "sit down" with my family's close friend, who happened to be the adult male leader of our Young Men's church group.

The first thing he did was hand me a cold pop and get me into the choir room, behind a closed door. Just the two of us. I remember staring at a picture of Jesus on the wall while he began molesting me, feeling me up and asking if I knew why I was in trouble.

He made it sound like his perverted actions happened in church all the time. It raised considerable doubt in me that this Jesus thing was real at all.

Because my family had branded me as a liar, no one believed me when I finally found enough courage to tell my father what happened. I was on my own.

His assaults lasted for several years, and my thoughts about organized religion deteriorated with each attack. How could I have any good feelings about Christianity or even Jesus Christ after all these terrible experiences?

At home, I was still locked into the "Yes, sir!" and "No, ma'am," "Please," and "Thank you," routine. If I didn't comply, I was either slapped or got the belt.

In the midst of all this, I developed a system of faking being in fights by cutting myself or making my head bleed. I didn't know at that time that my efforts were attempts to exhibit a false bravado and find a way to cope with and somehow make sense of my out-of-control environment.

Finally, I was old enough to refuse the disgusting advances of my father's "friend." Still, the experiences only intensified my sense of confusion and feelings of low self-esteem. My natural sense of moral values was severely shaken. I had discovered that churches could harbor wolves in sheep's clothing. No wonder my sense of morality was growing more and more vague.

One place I could "hide" in those days was our choir. I loved the music, and I was good at singing second bass. In 1966 I became our church's Youth for Christ Leader.

It looked like I might have the aptitude for being a worship leader. But I would have to go to Seminary or Bible College to obtain a degree. It was time for me to take charge of my life. Where would my own decisions take me?

In visiting jails and prisons, I often ask inmates, "How many of you grew up knowing who your Mom and Dad were?" That's not to imply that a dysfunctional home is a reason people commit crimes and are incarcerated. However, dysfunctional home life is often part of the background of inmates.

Discussion Questions

1. How does God exercise His authority differently than humans?
2. Why can you trust God when people fail you?
3. When you experience fear or anger, what is it that you really want?
4. How does a right relationship with God meet these desires/needs?
5. How can God's desires become your desires?
6. Examine the following verses that speak to changing your desires to match God's desires: Galatians 5:16; Colossians 3:5; 1 John 2:17; Matthew 6:21; 1 Corinthians 6:12; Isaiah 26:8; 2nd Peter 1:4.
7. Make a list of some righteous and godly responses to fear and anger.
8. Discussion: consider how you may have thought and acted differently during difficult times because of what you've learned about the power and glory of the Lord Jesus.

*P*ut to death, therefore, whatever belongs to your earthly nature: sexual immorality, lust, evil desires and greed, which is idolatry." - Colossians 3:5

CHAPTER TWO

SLIPPING INTO DARKNESS
1968 - 1971

During the 1960s, living in El Cajon was such a wonderful time.

The week I graduated from El Cajon High School my mind was illed with a multitude of emotions. On the one hand, I wanted to eave home and separate myself from my dysfunctional family. On he other hand, I wasn't ready to join the Navy, Army, Marines or any military service. I'd seen enough of that already. My future was uncertain.

This same week I sat down with my parents. I wanted them to know I had met with our California Lakeside Southern Baptist Church pastor, Senior Pastor Reverend Ron Chandler. I felt drawn to attend California Baptist College in Riverside, California. My intent was to pursue a Music Ministry degree. At the meeting with Pastor Chandler, I explained my aspirations. I asked if he would give me a letter of recommendation that I could present to the College.

Not only did he agree to send a letter to the College, but he gave me a letter of recommendation I could carry with me. Also, my church sponsored my books the first year. I paid tuition and board by working at various odd jobs around campus.

My future was looking quite inviting. As I waited for the fall semester to begin, I signed up to cook at the Southern Baptist Retreat Center in Glorietta, New Mexico.

That summer, I had a great time in Glorietta and nearby Santa

Fe. Outings included smoking Swisher Sweets (cigars), eating Baby Ruth candy bars, and drinking Dr. Pepper sodas. Though it sound pretty tame, my soul's rebel attitude began emerging while I wa there. I attended very few conference seminars at the Center wher I cooked. However, I did enjoy dating the Southern Baptist girl who came from all over the nation to attend events at the Center.

I finished out the summer there in Glorietta, achieving Chef sta tus in the kitchen, receiving a Certificate of Completion that I hel on to for many years. In subsequent years, it opened multiple door for me to work in restaurants.

I had entered a new phase of my life. My desire to complete a Musi Ministry degree was more intense than ever. Oh, the grandiose dream of the young!

That first year of freedom felt so liberating. No more rules, n more getting hit. Thus started my education at a Christian institution

I did well the first year, so well I was placed on the basketbal squad and cross-country team. I also took up dirt bike riding and spent many hours at Huntington Beach and Newport Beach, in search of the perfect surfing wave.

Each time my family came for visits, our time together neve ended as well as it began. I decided I would gradually remov myself from their lives. As I started my sophomore year, my brother Donald, now discharged from the Navy, attended Sem inary with me.

It was during that year that I encountered some new life experi ences: alcohol and speed.

Our basketball coach was determined to push me to my ful potential on the basketball court.

"Take one of these," he said. I swallowed the little pill, not real izing what it was or what it would do to me. At the time, I couldn' have imagined how drug use would take hold of my life for years to come.

After taking the pills, I was in a daze, but ruthless on the basket ball floor. Just what my coach was looking for.

Those little white pills nudged me toward a dark spiritual path The high I got from them made me feel I could be the person I had always wanted to be.

The entire basketball team wore letterman's jackets, featuring

"California Baptist College," as we frequented a topless club where we proceeded to drink our fill of beer. On one visit, I drank so much I became unconscious. It was my first blackout. It wasn't pretty.

It was the middle of the night when the other guys dropped me off at my dorm room. By daybreak, there was puke all over the dorm room floor and my fellow ministerial students. That same day I would experience my first intervention. Some of the college's administrative officials tried to help me understand that my behavior could result in suspension from the college.

At that point in my life, I didn't realize I was walking away from my relationship with God. I didn't understand I was squandering the opportunity of a lifetime. My church and the people at California Baptist College loved me unconditionally. That's why they helped me go to college. But I didn't love me unconditionally. I didn't take their warning seriously. Within just a few weeks I drank again. Another blackout. So young, so naive so wretched.

They called me to the Administration Office. I was asked to leave.

I had entered another new phase of my life: addiction. I was completely in its grip. Whether I was unable or unwilling at that point to control my drinking, I don't know. I know that all the experiences I'd had with "church" up to that point made it easy to kick to the curb the faith in Jesus I had once professed.

By now, I had become the manager of a drive-in movie theater. I nonchalantly packed my bags and proceeded to rent a nearby room. Everything would be okay. I could simply work and party. Oh, the parties!

Enthusiasm for my new lifestyle was short-lived. My drinking was increasingly worse. It wasn't long before the movie theater fired me. Again, I did my best to shake off any hint of accountability. I had a plan. I flew to San Francisco to hang out with my big brother, Tom. Donald stayed at the Seminary and eventually earned his degree in Ministry Education.

Coming from a military family, Tom encouraged me to join the military. He followed in Dad's footsteps, becoming a submariner. My brother Donald served for four years right after high school on a destroyer in Manila. He then used the GI Bill to complete his Bachelor's Degree in Christian Education.

23

Because I had a fear of open water, I joined the U.S. Army. My US Army induction was scheduled for the summer of 1968. In the meantime, Tom let me hang out at his house.

Since I lived in San Francisco, I expected to be assigned to California's Fort Ord. Instead, I found myself on a plane headed to Fort Lewis Washington. It was there I experienced my first snowfall. I also experienced an atmosphere which was much like the one I had recently escaped: my home. Commands, barking, and yelling filled my days. My drill Sergeant sounded very much like my stepmother.

Discussion Questions

1. What place did God have in your life before you became an adult?
2. When you left your childhood home, what were some of your youthful aspirations?
3. Did God influence your dreams and decisions at that point of your life?
4. Were you introduced to drugs and alcohol before you left your home?
5. Initially, how did drugs and alcohol make you feel?
6. At what point did you lose control of alcohol/substance abuse?
7. Were there opportunities or other things you lost or gave up on during your first years on your own?
8. Looking back, do you believe God was working in your life, even though you weren't aware of His presence?
9. What place does God have in your life now?
10. What role would you like to have God play in your life right now?

*F*or I know the plans I have for you," declares the Lord, "plans to prosper you and not to harm you, plans to give you hope and a future. Then you will call on me and come and pray to me, and I will listen to you. You will seek me and find me when you seek me with all your heart. I will be found by you," declares the Lord, "and will bring you back from captivity. I will gather you from all the nations and places where I have banished you," declares the Lord, "and will bring you back to the place from which I carried you into exile." – Jeremiah 29:11-14

CHAPTER THREE

OUT OF CONTROL

As I have mentioned, my Dad was a 23-year WWII veteran who served on a submarine as an Engine Room Chief Petty Officer, E-7. For most of our youth, my siblings and I never saw our father for nine months out of each year. One summer, he spent most of his time at the Navy base in Vallejo, California. The submarine he was assigned to, USS Catfish, was being overhauled.

If my out-of-control drinking habit hadn't led to my dismissal from the Seminary, I probably wouldn't have enlisted in the Army. However, after being asked to leave the Seminary, I found myself adrift. My only friend, it seemed, was the California sunshine.

When my brother Tom encouraged me to join the military, I sensed that enlisting would give my life some direction. I completed basic Army training at Ft. Lewis, Washington, then was assigned to Advanced Infantry Training (AIT) at Ft. Huachuca in Sierra Vista, Arizona. AIT training prepared me to be a truck driver in Germany.

Since I enlisted in the Army, my military status was RA – Regular Army. I was obligated to serve three years, rather than the two-year service required for soldiers who were drafted into the Army at that time.

During training, I learned how to operate as a gun-carrying infantry Truck Driver in case I was sent to Viet Nam. In those days, the gun trucks were armored vehicles equipped with one or more weapons. They were used to escort military convoys in regions subject to ambush by Vietnamese guerrilla forces. During that training,

I knew my orders indicated I would be stationed in Germany. don't believe I felt the same pressure my peers experienced wher they knew they would be sent to Vietnam as Combat Infantrymen

After arriving at my post in Germany, the Intelligenc Sergeant discovered I could type. He needed a legal clerk. Witr my educational experience at California Baptist College (now California Baptist University), the Sergeant believed I was capabl of taking on the duties of a legal clerk.

It surprised me that I loved working at the Army Headquarter in Germany. The challenge of learning the Uniform Code of Mili tary Justice (UCMJ) was rewarding. I rose through the ranks from a Private (E-2) to Sergeant (E-5) by working hard and studying for the test that would qualify me to be an NCO (Non-Commissionec Officer).

One of my duties was serving as the Colonel's APC (armorec personnel carrier) driver. An APC is a broad type of armored mil itary vehicle designed to transport personnel and equipment ir combat zones. They were sometimes called "battle taxis" or "battl buses."

The vehicle I drove was mounted with an M60 and M50. Th M60 is the official United States Machine Gun, part of a family o American general-purpose machines guns firing Caliber 7.62mn cartridges.

The M50 features six 106mm manually loaded M40 recoilless rifles, which can be fired in rapid succession against single targets.

I had to learn how to maintain and take care of the APC vehicle in case I needed to transport the head of our Battalior during war activities. In addition to qualifying in how to use and maintain these weapons, I was also trained to use a 45 calibe sidearm.

Other duties included traveling to Brigade Headquarters ir Frankfurt, Germany, for training in how to send and receive Morse Code messages from the Command APCs. All these new activities made service in the Army both challenging and exciting.

While my daytime hours in Germany were filled with a mix o training and assigned duties, I still found time in the evening tc satisfy my desire to consume alcohol. In the military, alcohol wa cheap and plentiful. When I acquired a Volkswagen I could use tc travel to Frankfurt after work, I soon found that the whole of Europe was my playground.

An important turning point in my life took place at that time. I experimented with a smoking pipe filled with hashish mixed with nicotine. My curiosity was drawing me into the military drug scene. I quickly learned how to support my drug habit by selling small amounts of drugs. That practice led to weekend forays in Munich, Hamburg, Amsterdam, even the island of Ibiza and Majorca, Spain.

I was accumulating endless stories of partying and drug dealing. Eventually, I found a pub with a potential hiding spot, away from the mainline GI discotheques. After being asked to work as a DJ (disc jockey) on weekends, I experienced some great times away from my post.

My downfall in all of this is something familiar to most drug dealers: an overwhelming sense of pride. It was false pride. The idea that I would change my ways when I was released from the Army was also mistaken.

The period of 1968-1971 was America's Age of Aquarius. I felt I was missing out on all that "fun." I had a fiancé in the states and a girlfriend from the German countryside. I told myself I was having the best of times. But inside I knew I was sacrificing my integrity and forsaking the Christian principles I had once adopted.

By the time I was released from the Army, I was being investigated for drug dealing and other related activities. It happened right before arriving at my birth mother's house in Los Angeles. I had a pipe laced with a small amount of LSD, a gift from a fellow soldier. Though I believed it was well hidden, it was discovered. On my last day of service I was busted from E-5 to E-4. My military service was still honorable, but it was a brutal reminder that every choice has a consequence. In spite of it all, I made it to my birth mother's home.

I'm not at all proud of how my military service ended, getting busted for drug possession. Looking back, it helps me understand why I went full bore into the drug scene and outlaw world of Los Angeles on the heels of my military service.

I've often been asked if I could give an example of God saving my life without saying it was just luck or coincidence. This incident definitely fits that scenario.

After my release from the Army, I settled in Los Angeles instead of San Diego. My birth Mom, Mary Jane Johansen (now deceased) lived there. My protective older sister, Beverly Peratt, also lived there at the time.

The problem was, I came to Los Angeles quasi addicted, selling off the 40 pounds of hashish I had sent home by mail. At that point in my life, I was on an addiction run of barbiturates (commonly called "Reds" or the pharma name Seconal). A keg of them consisted of 1,000 pills.

I continued in the throes of addiction when my family moved to Mom's birth town of Illiopolis, Illinois. That left me couch surfing on the couch's of welfare moms, dealing small amounts of pot and pills.

During this period, I purchased a keg of Seconal. After ingesting some to test them, I discovered they were very low in the barbiturate affect. This batch had been cut and repackaged as good product.

In my addictive state, I was totally mad, not capable of much logic. When I was in the Army, stationed in Europe, most of my hashish connections made good on any returned product. In my best addictive thinking I knew I had to go back to East Los Angeles or Compton (not sure which one) and confront this dealer to get uncut product or my money back.

I would soon find that this drug deal had little similarity to what I experienced in Europe. This Seconal dealer operated out of a Chicano-fortified house that was guarded in the front and back with pretty tough renegades.

It was the middle of the day and sunny Southern California would have been beautiful, but my anger blinded me to everything else but my insane mission. I couldn't find any of my biker connections to go with me, so I asked two of my buyers to accompany me. Unbeknownst to me, they had just ingested tabs of high-grade Orange Sunshine LSD. I had to borrow my brother-in-law's car to make the trip, and off we go on an adventure!

I was not packing iron (guns) but had a bat I planned to carry up to the door. My thought was, if the guards could be distracted, then I would demand being honored with good product.

To my surprise, no guards stood at the door. As soon as I opened the door, wow! Things started happening!

The moment the door swung open, I swear the biggest Latino dude I've ever seen in my life roared at me: "Get off my property!"

Even though this guy was intimidating, I was determined to get what I came for. And I had backup. I proceeded to get my bat ready, then turned to look at my friends. They were rolling on the ground, so stoned from the LSD they were worthless.

I wasn't going to give up. "You cut that keg and I want my money back!" I brandished my bat.

Not only did that Latino guy knock me off the porch, I heard him say, "Come on fellas, let's teach these white boys not to come to our part of town acting like they own it!"

The chase was on. My bat went flying. I had to run and grab both my "backups" and race some two blocks to the car. All I could think of as we ran was to use the Army Infantry training that taught me how to zig-zag, then run on the opposite side of the block.

But bullets were flying. Soon I felt a burning right below my groin area. I was bleeding down my leg. I experienced such pain as I never felt in my life.

We reached the car, scrambled into it and I started driving. We only drove for two blocks before I crashed my brother-in-law's car into two other vehicles.

Within seconds the Los Angeles Police were on the scene. Before I realized what was happening, the Chicanos were calmly walking back to their hood and my LSD intoxicated "backups" were nowhere to be seen.

The police issued me a ticket. I refused an ambulance. I had connections who stitched me up. Thankfully, the bullet had missed my groin, leaving me with an ugly bright red scar running across my leg.

But the pain wasn't over. I had to face the car owner's wrath and the disappointment of my brother-in-law and sister. And I gave up any hope of recovering the money for the drugs.

This is just one recounting of so many incidents that left me thinking how lucky I was. Now I know it was divine intervention that kept me from being killed as a result of my dangerous addictive thinking.

This incident took place just five years after I first enrolled in

Seminary. Such a contrast in my behavior. Doesn't take long to get involved with things way beyond the lifestyle we grew up with, right?

Are you thinking, "Yeah, I remember times like that in my own life. . .?"

It saddens me now to realize what a gift my new family – my birth mom's family – was. I'm sorry to say I didn't use my "older brother" status to offer much wisdom. My time with them was deeply tainted by drug use and alcohol.

Today, I work at redeeming some of the darkness I walked in during my time in the Army. I participate in most local American Legion activities, including serving for a time as Chaplain of the Legion Riders, Post 15, Sioux Falls, South Dakota. My battle with cancer forced me to step down from the chaplain role.

I have blessed bikes and regularly visited the Sioux Falls Veteran's Administration (VA) Hospital to pray with men and women in need. Other volunteer service includes completing training through ASSIST (Applied Suicide Intervention Skills Training) to respond to behaviors related to potential suicide. As a volunteer safeTALK (Suicide Alertness for Everyone) trainer, I give at least two annual three-hour presentations on Native American reservations in Nebraska and South Dakota.

Patriotism runs strong in my blood, which is why I fly a lighted American flag in my yard along with a metal replica of a soldier on bended knee. I also display an American flag on my Harley Davidson motorcycle, including for all national events.

While I served in the United States Army, I may have been a rebel. However, in the long run, I never gave up my faith in God and country. I am a very proud Christian Chaplain today.

Discussion Questions

1. Did you serve in the military at any time?
2. How did that experience impact your life? Positively? Negatively?
3. Looking back, what would you change about your behavior while you were in the military?
4. Whether or not you served in the military, are there things you wish you could change about your behavior during your first years away from home?
5. Since none of us can change the past, what steps can you take to resolve/redeem a time in your life when your behavior was unacceptable?
6. How does God redeem a wicked past?
7. What does God's forgiveness look like in your life?
8. Is there anything in your past that you believe God cannot forgive?
9. Why is God's forgiveness so important?
10. How has God used your past to change your understanding of life and living in a godly manner?

The Lord will scatter you among the peoples, and only a few of you will survive among the nations to which the Lord will drive you. There you will worship man-made gods of wood and stone, which cannot see or hear or eat or smell. But if from there you seek the Lord your God, you will find him if you seek him with all your heart and with all your soul. When you are in distress and all these things have happened to you, then in later days you will return to the Lord your God and obey him. For the Lord your God is a merciful God; he will not abandon or destroy you or forget the covenant with your ancestors, which he confirmed to them by oath." – Deuteronomy 4:27-31

CHAPTER FOUR

NASTY AL

After being released from the United States Army, I came home from Germany to live in Los Angeles.

At that time, the 1970s, California had beautiful weather, lots of free concerts, and many pretty people.

While I was happy to be released from the military, I had mixed emotions. When you're trained in the infantry to go to war and then don't go to war, there's a deep sense that something is missing.

Like the majority of Vietnam era veterans, I came home to a nation that wasn't interested in organizing a parade for us. At the time, the nation was seriously divided by the debate over the Vietnam war. Instead of the parades and hero's greeting World War II veterans had come home to, we found people cursing at us, spitting on our uniforms, and calling us baby killers. I was told I should burn my uniform.

I settled in Los Angeles because that's where my birth mother lived. What a mix of emotions I experienced when I found I had three new brothers and two new sisters. From the beginning to this present day, we are a very loving family.

However, I wasn't the most sterling addition to this family. In addition to an Army brother returning home (me), my new family now had an alcoholic and drug dealer in their midst. Before I arrived home, I sent some packages ahead of me.

Yes, I was already dealing drugs. I had smuggled 40 pounds of hashish. Instead of presents from Germany, Amsterdam, or Spain, I brought drugs. Those first few weeks after I came home were filled with parties with my new brothers and sisters. And boy, did we party!

My birth mother, whom I came to know and dearly love, didn't mind that I drank. She also drank. I learned that most of my adult family used alcohol, too.

I didn't stop drinking, but I invested some of my money in a barbiturate purchase from a local motorcycle club. In no time, I found myself enamored with their lifestyle of drinking, drugging, and partying.

Shortly after I became involved with this group, my family moved back to Illinois. The door was wide open for me to move into the motorcycle club's clubhouse.

I didn't hesitate to begin making runs with them to Tijuana. My smuggling career was underway. It never occurred to me that I was an international smuggler, bringing pills, LSD, marijuana, and whatever was available across the border. I was willing to smuggle anything that brought money to the club and me.

At this same time, I linked up with my high school sweetheart. Together we used drugs. Eventually, she became pregnant. We named our daughter Tuesday. Her brief life was ended when she was accidentally smothered with blankets. I blamed my girlfriend, as only a functional alcoholic would. I attempted to soothe my intense grief with drugs.

After our daughter's death, I moved to Niland, California. During World War II, weapons testing was conducted there near the Salton Sea. The testing site closed in the early 1970s. The abandoned ammo bunkers left behind made a great place to live.

Nearby, the sulfur springs became a nighttime refuge. It was there that I drank Boone's Farm wine. The practice was intended to drown the sorrow of losing my daughter. Instead, it caused me to howl at the moon in my grief.

During the six months that I lived in that desert area, I became convinced that I should kill my daughter's birth mother. I was certain that she carried a lot of blame for the direction my adult life had taken.

While God healed my heart during that period and removed

any further thought of harming her, alcohol and drugs claimed my soul. My drunkenness and attempts to numb myself through drug use were sinful. I know now I should have turned to God in my grief, drawn closer to him instead of moving even further away.

You can never combine sin (alcohol and drugs) with God. It just doesn't work. At that stage of my life, I wanted the booze and drugs more than I wanted God. It seemed to ease my pain, and help me escape the reality of my empty life.

My aching heart drew me to Illinois to visit my family. While I was there, I worked on local farms. Most nights, I drank and drugged myself to sleep with a mix of alcohol, barbiturates (sleep-inducing drugs), and marijuana.

Before I left California, I met a young lady, Teresa, in El Cajon. All the while I was in Illinois, I called Teresa, telling her again and again how I planned to return to El Cajon and date her. Little did I know this was the beginning of what has become a more than 45-year relationship. Our journey would take us through three years of a hippy lifestyle and 42 years of marriage. What a woman to put up with me! She's a genuine saint.

When I began dating Teresa, she was only 15, and I was 25. This was the "hippie" era, and her family made no objection to our relationship. Two weeks after Teresa and I met, we moved in together. Her parents made no effort to deter or stop us. Her family was very dysfunctional (her mother had become a witch), so there was no condemnation of our lifestyle. I would soon learn that Teresa had a background of moral injury from rape, stalking, and abuse by a family-in-law. We had both experienced a lot of trauma. We were comfortable with each other.

Because of my lifestyle, my language was pretty rough at this stage of my life. I had nasty thoughts, a nasty mouth, and my friends started to say, "No one can out-nasty Nasty Al." I constantly cussed and made terrible sexual innuendos toward women. Now I see that my soul was calloused and hard from all the evil choices and situations I exposed myself to. I continually gave in to my passion for sinning.

Once I returned to El Cajon, I lost no time before prospecting for a biker group. My motive was to help them establish a network of users.

That didn't last long because the Federal Government got involved, breaking up the biker group after they committed a very violent crime. Thankfully, I wasn't involved in the incident. I didn't realize it at the time, but God had redirected my path that night as a means of protecting me.

Still, it wasn't long before I began dealing drugs again in Los Angeles. The outlaw bikers I hung out with got mixed up in a terrible beating incident that led to someone's death. When it occurred, I was either too drunk or too high to participate or choose to say no. As I look back on the event, I recognize that, had I taken part in the crime, I could easily have been among the guys who ended up doing long stretches of time for it.

There was no big falling out with that group, but after the beating incident, I returned to my hometown of San Diego.

After all the gang breakups I experienced in 1973, Teresa, me, and an old school buddy of mine decided we'd start our own smuggling operation. We planned to bring drugs in from Mexico.

We started with kilos of marijuana, then moved to cocaine. Eventually, I turned to smuggling heroin. For my own drug use, I was still into drinking and using lots of marijuana. It didn't take long for me to become deeply involved in Mexico's Tijuana drug trade.

Before I knew it, I was behind on some drug payments. That led me to agree to smuggle a pound of heroin across the border to pay off my debt. It wasn't common for drug dealers, like my Mexican connection, to agree to let me pay off the money I owed him by smuggling heroin. But it seemed like a perfect solution for me. I hadn't used heroin at that point and wasn't addicted to it.

By 1974 the California State Narcotics and Federal Drug Enforcement Agency set me up for a sting. What had seemed a perfect solution to paying for the cocaine I was using resulted in doing time at the San Diego County Jail. Before it was all over, I was sentenced to five-to-life in the California Prison System.

At Chino State Prison, a classification unit, officials made the decision as to whether inmates were sent to Soledad, San Quentin or Folsom Prison.

During my time in Chino, they decided I was just a drug dealer and not a violent offender. If I could get off the drugs they put me on, I would be allowed to go to Fire Camp. There I would be trained to help fight fires or be deployed to help with other types of major emergencies in California like floods or earthquakes.

I knew the Fire Camp food was better, and I always liked to work. I got off the State's drugs and spent time fighting fires for the state of California while I served my sentence. I completed nearly 1 months in the California prison system.

Then California Governor Jerry Brown helped me dodge the bus to San Quentin. At that time, Brown recommended a treatment setting in a separate prison for first time offenders, like myself. Since had a five-to-life sentence, the California Department of Corrections had to agree to allow me to participate in this program. The outcome was my release after serving three years in prison. I was also given a three-year parole.

That three-year Chino State Prison sentence was a significant wake-up call for me. I believe God sometimes gives us breaks to help us determine where we are in life and where we want to go. However, my guilty conscience did little to affect this stubborn, prideful man.

On this side of addiction, it's hard to believe how far the power of drug addiction pushes addicts like me. In order to obtain and use drugs, I began sinking to incredible levels of scheming and deceit, exhibiting behaviors that today totally baffle me.

Once I was released, I decided to try this drug, heroin, that had landed me in prison. What was all the hoopla about? I had no intention of listening to the people who had warned me, "Don't try heroin! Not you! You'll be addicted very shortly." Usually, if you tell me what to do, I do the opposite.

I tried heroin. And I didn't like it, I loved it!

I was holding down a regular job, working on construction, to keep the parole authorities happy. At the same time, chipping away at my new drug of choice, heroin, I was becoming what is known as a "Chippie," using drugs every weekend.

Alcohol and marijuana use were tolerated by parole authorities at that time. That allowed me to purchase urine from anyone who just used those stimulants and provide a "clean" urine sample each time I checked in with my parole officer.

Little by little I was being drawn into the secret society of "junkies," becoming way too enamored with this group. Prior to that time I had read about junkies, knew a few, but had never before become so involved with them.

Between my $200/day drug use and the daily cost of Teresa's addiction, no amount of pawning or shoplifting was going to support our drug habits. Because Teresa was my wife, life partner, and mother of my children, prostitution was off the table.

As part of my three-year parole agreement, I couldn't leave the city limits of San Diego. However, I had to have heroin. My solution was to go back to Mexico. In Tijuana, past the bullring on the edge of town towards the ocean, and up in the hills of Tijuana was the area known as the barrio, a polite term for "hood."

I convinced my past connection to front me enough heroin that I could support both my and Teresa's habits and make enough to satisfy his business need for making money. All I cared about was getting my heroin.

I held down my job, but not very well. Just enough to fake it.

In the throes of addiction, my bride and I only trusted each other. She accompanied me when I went down south, packaging the baggies that I would eventually swallow before we crossed the border.

Put your index finger to your thumb. That was our measuring tool to not go over that amount of heroin in a triple wrapped American made balloon. Otherwise, the heroin-filled baggies choked me. If that occurred while I was swallowing them, someone on the ready would hit me in the back to force the stuck balloon out of my throat.

Once we crossed back into California, we quickly made our way to a gas station bathroom so I could throw up the baggies. Vomit, regurgitation. Graphic? You bet. That was before x-ray machines were used. Of course, we knew we couldn't use condoms as those dissolved in the acidity of stomach fluids. We determined that 37 was the largest number of baggies my throat and stomach could tolerate.

Now, all 37 never came out of my stomach. There were times when my intestines would become lodged with one or more baggies.

Then, it was a combination of withdrawing or "kicking" the habit just long enough to have a bowel movement, then back to shooting heroin until the next time.

This baffling behavior went on every week for a full year. We borrowed different cars to beat the Border Patrol system. I paid off a few agents, and even paid the $300 charge to have a green card worker smuggle the drugs across.

Cunning actions, baffling behavior, insidious habits, and a powerful demand for the drug. That is the story of addiction.

I experienced an eight-year love affair with heroin, ranging between not using for some time to being completely strung out.

So, what finally derailed this crazy ride? I paid $25 for a urine sample, for the first time obtaining it from a woman. For weeks, each time I had to go in to the Parole Office, I carried the clean sample with me, emptying it into the lab container they gave me in the bathroom. It had worked beautifully.

Generally, a few minutes after providing the sample, I was dismissed in short order. But this time, I was escorted to the Parole Officer and directed to have a seat in the chair in front of his desk. My gut told me something was up. I made my best effort to remain calm and cool.

"Mr. Peratt, how are you doing?" Not an unusual question.

"I'm fine." The officer didn't say a word. Just stared hard at me.

"It appears, Mr. Peratt, that you are pregnant."

I felt the blood drain from my face. Busted. There was no use trying to maintain the ruse I had employed for so long. I courteously described the process I had used to escape detection.

Aah! The ways our God gets us to make choices that help us can be painful. However, I know now that, if I hadn't been caught, sooner or later one heroin balloon was bound to break and thus end my life.

Treatment was recommended and, again, I lied my way through a simple outreach program. After all the antics, I was still "not ready" to quit my lifestyle.

What a journey addiction can be, and the family suffers through it and beyond!

Once I finally finished what was required of me, it would be nearly 15 years before authorities caught up to me again. In the meantime, I was trying to preserve my marriage.

It was after my release from Chino prison in 1977 that methamphetamine came into our home. My wife loved speed. I'm not saying I never used it, but only occasionally.

I was growing high THC marijuana in the forests outside San

Diego then. The drug that put me in the penal system, heroin, was making my life much worse. For nearly eight years, I was addicted to heroin. It seemed each time I was able to tear myself away from heroin use, some kind of dilemma took over my life, and I ran back to the drug and alcohol world.

Teresa and I weren't involved in any crimes at that point. It was during this period of our lives that our son was born. We were overjoyed at his birth. However, between drugs and our chaotic lifestyle, Teresa and I slowly drifted away from one another.

Among the things we experienced then was the abuse of our son by my wife's nephew. When Teresa and I ended up having a major fight, and she picked up two butcher knives, I knew something had to change. I grabbed my next paycheck, our son, and moved to South Dakota. I'd heard there were little or no drugs there at that time.

But it didn't take me long to connect with South Dakota's drug scene. Before I knew it, Teresa followed me to the Dakotas. We reconciled and soon settled back into our drug-dealing lifestyle. At the same time, I tended bar in a club, and she danced there. Financially, it was a lucrative time for us.

Discussion Questions

1. How do self-deception and the practice of deceiving others go hand-in-hand?
2. Do we find long-lasting peace through a life of deception?
3. Can we find healing for life's hurts when we turn away from God?
4. Looking back, were there times when God gave you an opportunity to change your life?
5. Do you recognize points in your life when God was protecting you, even though you didn't know it at the time?
6. Does God ever give up on us when we reject him again and again?
7. Do you believe it's ever too late to choose a godly path in life?

*O*nly be careful, and watch yourselves closely so that you do not forget the things your eyes have seen or let them fade from your heart as long as you live. Teach them to your children and to their children after them. Remember the day you stood before the Lord your God at Horeb, when he said to me, "Assemble the people before me to hear my words so that they may learn to revere me as long as they live in the land and may teach them to their children." You came near and stood at the foot of the mountain while it blazed with fire to the very heavens, with black clouds and deep darkness. Then the Lord spoke to you out of the fire. You heard the sound of words but saw no form; there was only a voice." – Deuteronomy 4:9-12

CHAPTER FIVE

STING OPERATION

Even though we left the State of California behind, once we settled in South Dakota, Teresa and I quickly became immersed in the same lifestyle we had known in California: drugs and alcohol. Our drug sales involved cocaine, psylocybin mushrooms, marijuana, methamphetamine and LSD.

By 1987, we were trafficking illegal drugs in the Rapid City area to the degree that our operation was the largest drug operation ever known in the State of South Dakota.

Like most drug addicts and dealers, we were pretty confident that we were getting away with our illicit activities. What we didn't know was that, in April 1987, law enforcement officials had set up an undercover drug operation out of a building, a t-shirt store, on Rapid City's Canyon Lake Drive. Their intent was to draw drug dealers into the store to transact drug sales and then snare those involved in the local drug sale network.

It was at that same time, April 1987, when I caught the attention of federal officials after having a conversation with a CI (confidential informant) about buying and selling meth. He bought meth from me. Over the next 21 months, law enforcement officers remained undercover, gathering evidence about drug deals involving me and 42 other people.

In November 1989, in the largest drug bust in South Dakota since the 1970s, I was one of 43 arrested. The South Dakota Grand Jury indicted me on seven counts of Distribution of a Controlled

Substance and Conspiracy to Distribute a Controlled Substance. I found guilty, I was facing a maximum penalty of 20 years in pris on for each charge and a $250,000 fine for each distribution and conspiracy charge.

In January 1990, the Rapid City Journal headline read, "City sting operation nets 43 drug arrests." The story explained that "suspects were videotaped by concealed camera as they sold drug to undercover agents in the store."

While awaiting sentencing, I was held at the South Dakota State Penitentiary (SDSP) in Sioux Falls. Inmates call it "The Hill."

After enjoying a drug-addicted lifestyle, evading the law by slipping through one loophole after another, I was finally confronted with the reality of the cold, steel bars of my prison cell. Before this anytime I found myself doing time, I had summoned every ounce of imagination and determination to avoid acknowledging where my addictive behaviors were taking me.

Now there was a possibility I could serve as much as 40 years. could also find myself facing conviction as a habitual offender. Was it possible I would spend the rest of my life behind bars?

I felt I'd been dealt a death blow. I was suffering physically from liver disease brought on by my drug habits. Physically, I had never felt so spent. Morally, psychologically, and spiritually I was beyond empty

In November 1989, as I lay on my cot in SDSP's Orientation/ Indoctrination (O&I) unit, I was withdrawing from drugs. I wasn' sure if it was a hallucination, but I heard a lonely, wavering voice softly singing. "Jesus loves me, this I know. For the Bible tells me so . . ." The words were followed by the muffled sobs of an inmate I knew exactly what he was experiencing: Missing his home or life on the outside. Crying into his pillow so others wouldn't make fur of him.

There was no escape. I finally recognized it. I was trapped Caught red handed. All the weight of past violations began settling on me like a lead suit. As the consequences of all my past actions overtook me, it brought me to my knees.

"Lord." I breathed the word I had barely thought about for years. "My family."

Teresa and our kids were back in California, living with her parents. Teresa was fighting her own battle with drug use. Our marriage had been anything but ideal. But I loved her, loved my kids. What would happen to them now? They might be okay, but I would be of no help to them. Not for a long time. Maybe never.

I bowed my head. It was time to repent. Time to turn away from the "pleasures" that were killing me, and my family. I had never needed God's forgiveness, his help and his strength more than I did right then.

"God, no matter what kind of sentence I receive, I am ready to serve you." My whispered words were steeped in sorrow, remorse for past actions, and determination to begin allowing God to come back into my life. I wanted to change. How could I possibly begin?

The next day, I began journaling, a practice that prisoners are encouraged to learn. By putting on paper some of the confusion and illusion that had overtaken my life over 37 years, I began seeing some things that strengthened my desire for a change of heart. That awakening helped shape my life into the person I am today.

There's an unwritten law amongst inmates that, when the hammer falls, you don't ask your wife/woman to wait for you. That isn't fair to them.

Even though inside you desperately want them to stay with you, stand beside you through all your pain, you release them to go on their way. You can't hold onto them. That only hurts them. If at the end of your sentence, they're still waiting for you, you're lucky.

I didn't want Teresa to recognize my desperation, my anguish over the thought of losing her and my kids. I made my call to her as short as I could. "I don't know what's gonna' happen, babe. Don't worry about me. Do what you gotta' do."

The words brought some kind of relief and peace, which I hadn't experienced for a long, long time. I wasn't putting the burden of my sentence on her. But the idea that I'd probably lose the only woman I ever really loved tore me up. My desolate surroundings reminded me: things had changed. We both had to go on. I had to toughen up, face the consequences of my actions like a man.

One of my best skills at that point in my life was lying. I had learned it at a young age in order to protect myself and get what I wanted, at least some of the time. I attempted to bury the lingering pain that came from my stepmother's vicious discipline and scathing condemnations.

In General G. C. Marshall's book, "Soul Repair," I read that, "The soldier's heart, the soldier's spirit, the soldier's soul, are everything." My soul was fractured then and would be for a major portion of my life.

In Romans 7:19, Apostle Paul wrote, "For what I do is not the good I want to do; the evil I do not want to do, this I keep on doing." And Romans 7:23 says, "But I see another law at work in the members of my body, waging war against the law of my mind and making me a prisoner of the law of sin at work within my members."

These scriptures described me to a "T." My soul was lost, and I was slowly drifting into accepting the idea that I was doomed to live in sin and darkness, confusion, chaos and pain.

"Treatment" was required for inmates (addicts) like me. A trained counselor led our daily class, walking us through a maze of activities designed to transform our thoughts and behavior. The sting of incarceration still had me on a roller coaster of emotion. "Nasty Al" was usually in control at any given moment. The rebellious attitude that had dominated my life up to this point led me to taunt that counselor, twist or attack everything he said. I wasn't going to make it easy for that guy. My "classmates" pretty much kept silent, not giving any indication of how my behavior was affecting them. But they were talking to other inmates. Word quickly spread that "Nasty Al" was living up to his name.

At this same time, I started attending an Alcoholics Anonymous meeting called "New Beginnings." At this meeting I was re-introduced to a lifer called Reid Holiday. Reid was a lifer I first met through AA at South Dakota State Penitentiary (SDSP) in Sioux Falls. When we both ended up at the Medium Security facility, Mike Durfee State Penititeniary (MDSP) in Springfield, South Dakota, our friendship began to blossom. I had allowed Reid to get close to me as I started settling into prison, at least closer than anyone else. In the few weeks I had known him, he proved to be square with me, giving me good advice and behaving like a genuine friend. I respected him.

When Reid heard about my class time antics, he wasted no time in calling me on it.

"We're going for walk," Reid said, pointing me toward the running track out in the yard. I followed him.

"What the hell are you doing?" His question caught me off guard. I didn't answer or even look at him. Eyes straight ahead, I walked beside him.

"You're making that whole class mad," Reid said. "You and I both know that you can act like an a__hole and pretend you're a tough guy, but the truth is you're tired of all that, aren't you? You're tired of trying to always be tougher and smarter than the next guy. Tired of trying to stay ahead of somebody. Admit it, Al, you're miserable!"

For the next 90 minutes, Reid hammered me with question after question: Who's taking care of your wife now? Who's watching out for your kids? That's killing you, isn't it? What is your life going to be like for the next 25 to 30 years?

Those questions run through the mind of every inmate in every prison. But most of us won't allow ourselves to admit to our thoughts, or even consider answering those questions.

Reid asked me if there was anything I wanted to improve in my life. I proceeded to explain to him how all my life I sometimes had to defend myself by lying. After a couple laps around the track, I admitted I simply had a habit of lying.

Reid went on to explain that lying was a problem he once had in his own life. He, too, had experienced a lifetime of lying, cheating and conning people. I explained to him that I knew reversing this destructive habit may not be easy, but I wanted it to happen. I was sick of the lifestyle I'd been leading for over 20 years. I wanted to change, but I didn't know where to even start. And I wasn't sure I could change, that anything about me could be different.

When you've been doing drugs, for as many years as I had, and then you're locked up, your emotions are beyond raw. As I was sobering up, I wanted to feel something genuine again. I wanted that so bad.

But the only genuine emotion I began to recognize, one that I came to understand had been there for so long, was anger. It started sinking in that I had been and still was raging at life, raging at God. When I looked at my life journey, it felt like my parents had set me up to fail when they selfishly gave in to their own alcoholism. They walked away from me and my siblings, leaving us to get by the best we could.

When my twisted stepmother came into the picture, my anger only expanded. It seemed to me that she, and everything else in life, only beat me down. When my childhood fury led to being branded a liar, I embraced it. Maybe lying would get me through the maze of pain every facet of life seemed to hold. It was the first step toward my life of rebellion and revolt.

Now, I was facing the consequences of years of running from reality. In light of Reid's upbraiding, I had to admit, I was very tired of "Nasty Al."

As we walked around that track, Reid quoted the Bible, sharing John 8:32: "Then you will know the truth, and the truth shall set you free."

I could barely imagine living a life of truth. In my past there had been truthful, upstanding people. They made that lifestyle look so easy, like a piece of cake. That only made it harder for me to imagine how I could ever make that transition.

Reid didn't demand answers from me that afternoon. We finished our walk. He went on his way and I on mine.

A few weeks before our "talk," I received a Bible in the mail. My parents sent it to me, praying it would instill a desire to change my life. I began reading some of it. But every Sunday, when Reid stopped by my cell to invite me to church, I said, "No, thanks."

Reid wasn't one to give up. The Sunday after our talk, he came by my cell. "Peratt? Going to church today?"

"Yes." His eyes grew wide. He dropped the books he carried.

"Did you say yes?" I did. We went to church. I started reading the Bible more often, taking time to really think about what I read, allowing God to start breaking through the shell of hardness I had built. Once Reid realized I was serious about making some changes in my life, he began challenging me.

"You know all those people you've been lying to?" he asked. "Make a list for me."

I wrote out the list and gave it to him. I thought he would embrace me and tell me what a great job I had done. Instead he proceeded to have me explain each lie to him. Then he said I had to write a second list, go back to those same people and make amends.

I couldn't eat my popcorn that night. All I could think about was how embarrassing it was going to be to admit to those people that I lied to them.

It's humiliating to admit you lied. And I wanted to stop lying, but this seemed too extreme. At first.

I decided to do exactly what Reid instructed.

The next night was ice cream night. Woo-hoo! Ice cream is a favorite food in the penitentiary. In addition to enjoying a treat, this same night I could tell Reid, my AA sponsor, I had indeed gone back and to the best of my ability made amends to those people I had lied to. I was proud to show him my new list. Reid made no bones about telling me this list seemed to be shorter than the one he saw the day before. My! What a revelation!

It wasn't easy and there was a part of me that wanted to run away from this new behavior as fast as I could. But I knew where those steps would lead me. For two weeks I repeated the pattern of making a list of people I needed to be honest with.

This was not fun for me, yet I felt just a little glimmer of hope in my heart. Just maybe I could stop lying. It made me learn that principle of stop, and think, before talking.

On this side of those experiences, I know Reid knew what he was talking about. Pardoned and granted full clemency, my Christian brother, Reid, is now a productive member of society. When he was pardoned and released, I gave him a ride to work for a year, practicing "paying it forward." Reid is now married to a strong Christian lady and loves bow hunting, fishing and many outdoor activities. He is often asked to speak to others about how to achieve life changes through faith in God and walking our talk.

Discussion Questions

1. How does sin enslave people?
2. How do you know when you are being controlled by your emotions or circumstances rather than by God's Holy Spirit?
3. Can you recall a time when you reached a turning point in your life? How did you respond – by changing your life or by backing away from change?

*T*hen you shall know the truth and the truth will set you free." - John 8:32

CHAPTER SIX

COURT AND ACCOUNTABILITY

It should have been no surprise that God had mercy on me, even though I had utterly rebelled against Him for 17 years.

As the date for my sentencing approached, my resolve to let God redirect my paths grew deeper and more undeniable. I knew I couldn't promise anyone anything. I could just walk in the light God was providing as I worked through each day.

My attorney sent me a letter prior to sentencing. He made it clear that a guilty plea was virtually my only option once I went to court.

"I suppose I should touch upon appeal rights," my attorney wrote. "If any appeal is taken, the appeal must be commenced within thirty days following the Notice of Entry of Judgment. If you desire to take an appeal, I will require you notify me in writing by August 15. You and I both know it would be futile and imprudent to take an appeal. You cannot appeal a sentence that is lawful. Your sentence is not only lawful, from everything I'm aware of, but is significantly below the guideline sentence. I am sure you are aware of it and also aware it would not be wise to irritate Judge Battey by taking an appeal when our defense strategy has always been based upon a wiser design. Nonetheless, I need to make sure you know your appeal rights, and you may now forget about them."

When my sentencing date arrived, I did my best to stand before the judge with peace in my heart. I was confident that God was with me, and I was trusting him.

I wasn't exactly the same man they arrested weeks ago. God had begun answering my prayers to find a new way to live. I was learning the value of discipline, reading the Bible, regularly attending church, and AA meetings. I was genuinely seeking a new direction for my life.

Was it too late? Would the judge show any leniency, or would he determine that I was more likely to repeat past behaviors rather than make a genuine transformation? Would God answer my heartfelt prayer for mercy? Or had I drawn so much out of my mercy account that there was little left to allocate?

Amid the whirlwind of thoughts flooding my mind, I came back again and again to one solid foundation I had found. I wouldn't lie to the judge, for any reason. I was done with that habit. I had set my mind to accomplishing the challenging work of placing my feet on a new path. This was no time to waver from that commitment. No matter what happened in the courtroom that morning, I would be honest.

At this time, I had served one year of my sentence at South Dakota State Penitentiary. Now I was in Federal Court facing charges of leading a Continuing Criminal Enterprise (CCE) and Racketeering Influenced Corrupt Organization (RICO). Under the law, which is designed to specifically target organized crime, these charges can lead to paying huge fines and up to life imprisonment. Typically, harsh sentences are handed out for convicted operation leaders or supervisors like myself.

My entire future was on the line. They had hard evidence. No amount of scheming and lying would provide an escape. I reached deep inside myself to summon every scrap of serenity I could find. My heart was set on trusting God, allowing him to guide my steps.

As I entered the courtroom, it was comforting to see Teresa seated in one of the back rows of chairs. She had returned from California to be there for me.

The judge peered at me as I stood before him, awaiting his decision.

"This report tells me that, since your arrest, you've taken steps to alter your lifestyle," he said. I didn't answer. I had no desire to brag about or embellish the information he had in front of him.

"You're facing some severe charges, Mr. Peratt."

"Yes, sir. I'm very thankful that you took me out of the drug scene and brought me to prison." There was no point in pleading innocence or begging for mercy. The evidence was clear.

The judge was silent for what seemed an eternity.

"Based on what I know about your past history . . ." The words sent a chill through me.

"I'm going to give you an opportunity to prove yourself." I wasn't sure I understood.

"You were indicted on seven counts," the judge said. "I'm dismissing six of them. I'm also dismissing your fines." Hope and a joy I hadn't felt for so long – maybe ever – was rising inside me.

"I sentence you to four and one-half years, minus the time you've already served," the judge added. "This is concurrent with your state time. I'm giving you this chance, Mr. Peratt. But make no mistake. If I see you in my court again, it will not go well with you. What do you have to say for yourself?"

I could hardly believe my ears. A Federal sentence concurrent with a State sentence was virtually unheard of. What should I say? The old me would have gushed with words intended to manipulate and take advantage of what seemed too good to be true. But I was a different person now. I wouldn't lie. I couldn't lie anymore.

"I won't lie to you, Judge." I couldn't say I was completely changed. That wasn't true. Every day I fought the urge to give in to old behaviors. What I knew to be true was my determination to do my very best in changing my life. The judge gave me a quizzical look.

"I will continue doing everything I can to change my life."

My knees were weak. As I left the courtroom, I was still trying to grasp what had just happened. My determination to do what was right was already bringing blessings to my life. God had answered my prayers for mercy. I really was making good choices.

I couldn't wait to discuss this wonderful news with Teresa. She was as thrilled as I was to hear the judge's lenient sentence. Despite all we had been through, we loved each other. Being separated wasn't easy.

In the weeks that followed, each time I spoke with Teresa on the phone, I shared some things God was doing in my heart. She laughed at my words, thinking I was probably using some kind of code because the phone lines were tapped. Growing up in a household where she was forbidden to say anything about God, Teresa didn't understand the changes I experienced.

I never pushed her to join me on this new path, but I remained steadfast in trusting God to bring us through whatever lay ahead.

After my sentence was pronounced, I was transferred to a medium-security facility called Mike Durfee State Prison (MDSP). At this prison, I started looking around, seeing the beautiful environment around me. Formerly, this facility was a college. The "campus" is replete with trees, grass, and a much different atmosphere than I found in the maximum-security facility.

I continued attending church, studying my Bible, and attending AA meetings. Every day God spoke to me and showed me things about myself and the plan he had for me. It was a complete change from when my parents tried to beat bad behaviors out of me. Or in the military, where discipline should have brought out character flaws. I finally saw what a liar I had been. It was clear to me that my own decisions had led me down this dark, destructive path.

My initial decision to humble myself and turn from the practice of lying and trying to gain an advantage over others would prove to be an invaluable move.

As a new creation in Christ, I'm still quick to humble myself and allow God to lead me in his will and his way. The enemy always wants me to take the softer, easier way out of life's circumstances. In reality, the right way is sometimes the hardest way.

This principle of honesty is vital to those of us who never developed that discipline in our lives. It's time to turn our lives over to the care of our Higher Power, who is Jesus Christ, my Savior, my Lord.

Professionals tell us that, after the age of 16, habitual behavior is hard to change. I was one who thought I would never be able to change my drug and alcohol behavior, let alone a practice such as lying.

Sometimes we develop the habit of lying as a defense mechanism. As young people, we often hear that telling the truth makes things go easier on us. Then, when it doesn't go easier on us, we feel we were told a lie. It doesn't take a brain surgeon to determine that there's a 50-50 chance I'll avoid a beating or incarceration if someone believes my lie.

The problem is, once we start lying, our lives become a little darker with each untruth. Each deception results in a few more clouds. Each innuendo deepens our inclination toward deceitful action. More embellishments lead to even more lies.

I have found that my Bible tells me many truths and encourages me not to lie. Lies break relationships, including our relationship with God. Lies cause so many problems for us.

Today, as I speak to recovering addicts in treatment centers, I share this fundamental principle that I began sharing in 1989. Any behavior can be changed if you're willing to put in the work. It has to come from deep within, that spiritual element, that soul thing.

For the person reading this book, turn from the thought that there is no hope for you. Jesus is our hope. That doesn't mean you don't have to do the hard work. Taking a new path is nothing that comes easy. Easy Street is the wrong street. Hard Work Street is the right street.

May God grant you the grace to find direction and find the truth in your life.

Discussion Questions

1. Do you expect to experience God's mercy?
2. What does God's Word say about His thoughts toward you?
3. Do you believe God has played any role in the positive and/ or negative elements of your life?
4. Are you willing to seek God's direction for your life and how can you accomplish that?
5. Are you willing to follow his leading when He reveals areas of your life that need to change?
6. What causes you to be willing to allow God to change and heal you?
7. What do you want in life more than anything else?
8. What are some ways you can stay focused on God and His priorities for your life?
9. What brings Christians the "peace that passeth all understanding?" (Phillipians 4:7)

*T*he boy Samuel ministered before the Lord under Eli. In those days the word of the Lord was rare; there were not many visions.

One night Eli, whose eyes were becoming so weak that he could barely see, was lying down in his usual place. The lamp of God had not yet gone out, and Samuel was lying down in the house of the Lord, where the ark of God was. Then the Lord called Samuel.

Samuel answered, "Here I am." And he ran to Eli and said, "Here I am; you called me."

But Eli said, "I did not call; go back and lie down." So he went and lay down.

Again the Lord called, "Samuel!" And Samuel got up and went to Eli and said, "Here I am; you called me."

"My son," Eli said, "I did not call; go back and lie down."

Now Samuel did not yet know the Lord: The word of the Lord had not yet been revealed to him.

A third time the Lord called, "Samuel!" And Samuel got up and went to Eli and said, "Here I am; you called me."

Then Eli realized that the Lord was calling the boy. So Eli told Samuel, "Go and lie down, and if he calls you, say, 'Speak, Lord, for your servant is listening.'" So Samuel went and lay down in his place.

The Lord came and stood there, calling as at the other times, "Samuel! Samuel!"

Then Samuel said, "Speak, for your servant is listening."
– 1 Samuel 3:1-10

CHAPTER SEVEN

HUMBLE AND TRUSTING: IS THAT ME?

When I finally set my heart on taking a new path in life, it was not easy to determine where to begin.

With the encouragement of my Christian brother and prison AA sponsor, Reid, I decided to stop lying to people. In the beginning, to help me be accountable for that decision, Reid had me make a weekly list of anyone I had lied to. After reviewing the list, he instructed me to go to each person, acknowledge that I lied and make it right with them.

That's a tall order. It requires humility, trust in God, and working through a process of change. I had to stop looking at others with the notion that I should find out what I could take from them. It was time to find out how to help others, not cheat them.

I started looking at every aspect of my life, including my smoking habit. I decided to give my cigarettes away. By not smoking, I saved quite a bit of money, which my wife needed to help take care of her while I was incarcerated.

After a time, my habit of cursing began to fade. My heart and mind were changing. Cursing no longer fit me.

By going to church and spending time reading and studying the Bible, my thoughts were changing. I was able to take an honest look at the things I had done, the lifestyle I had adopted. I was finding great peace in leaving my rebellious past behind and moving forward.

Over the 3½ years I was in prison, I was determined to do all I could to prepare myself for the day I was released. I completed a business degree and became certified as a paralegal. I fully immersed myself in completing the 12 Steps of Alcoholics Anonymous.

By the time I was up for parole, I didn't want to leave. I was involved in church and Bible studies. I had a network of trusted friends and mentors.

Throughout this time of change, some wanted to test me. That's true for nearly every ex-con. Sometime, somewhere, someone will seek to find out what we're made of. That's okay. God knows, and I know what's inside. A lifetime of honoring God and doing what's right will be our testimony.

No matter how sincere we are about serving God while we're behind the walls, the real test of our commitment comes when we're released. Don't kid yourself: regaining the freedom to make our own choices will bring plenty of temptation. Each day we have to set our heart and mind on making the right choice, one day, one hour, one minute at a time.

One of the best things we can do when we're released is to find someone who can hold us accountable. For me, that was a Narcotics Anonymous sponsor. The same day I was released, my sponsor picked me up for an evening meeting. As much as I wanted to spend that time with my family, doing ordinary things I couldn't do on the inside, I knew accountability had to be a priority.

Over the years, I have faithfully attended both NA and AA (Alcoholics Anonymous) meetings, working wholeheartedly to support the change inside me. The encouragement and support of those men who stood beside me were so crucial to my recovery.

Many of us fail to recognize the value of developing a spiritual foundation as we take steps on a new path. Without learning about and making God's principles for living part of our lifestyle, we'll either be sucked back into old life patterns or drawn into new destructive obsessions. That's not just true for those of us in recovery. It's a fact for every person on earth. We need the spiritual foundation God provides if we want to build a stable new life.

Don't get me wrong; initially, these changes are hard. We never know what a new day brings. Moving away from what was so familiar in our lives can be intimidating, overwhelming. We shouldn't try to look too far into the future. For today we can put one foot in front of the other, moving forward on this new path. I promise, if we do that, we soon see the results of our commitment. Our actions, whether good or bad, create a reaction. That's guaranteed.

My wife wasn't even sure I could accomplish what I had set my mind to achieve. I wasn't the same man who had gone into prison a couple years earlier. She often wondered, "Who is this person?"

I knew that if I didn't commit to changing, I would become a serial killer or be locked away in prison for the rest of my life. The dishonest thought patterns I had established could only take me down a dark path.

And the change had to go all the way through me. I had always been good at adapting to my environment. I knew how to play different roles, fit in with different groups. Any of us can put on an outward show. But is there a change in our hearts? Does our commitment to a new life go deeper than just the words we say?

Discussion Questions

1. Do you believe you have achieved genuine change in your life? Why do you believe that?
2. What evidence of change do you see in yourself?
3. Have you accepted that change is often difficult for anyone?
4. What makes it worth the effort for you to work at changing your life?
5. Do you have a God-centered focus that helps guide you to positive/productive changes?
6. What steps do you take to develop/maintain your relationship with God?
7. Why are you sometimes overcome by temptation?
8. Are there sinful areas of your life that you're not willing to change? Why?

There is a time for everything, and a season for every activity under heaven . . . A time to weep and a time to laugh, a time to mourn and a time to dance." Ecclesiastes 3: 1, 4

The butterfly is a symbol of hope, the symbol of new life and the symbol of those who are bereaved. Before it becomes a butterfly, though, it must spend time in a cocoon.

We might be tempted to help release the butterfly from her cocoon. It is human nature to want to assist, but if we do, she will fall to the ground and die. By her struggle to free herself, she strengthens her wings enough to survive and fly.

Grief is certainly like this process. We feel ugly, we change, we hide, we sometimes spin a cocoon around ourselves. It takes a long time. There is a difference, however. Others may help us as we struggle. We need not do it all alone as the butterfly does, but the ultimate responsibility is ours.

We have to grieve, hurt, cry, be angry and struggle to free ourselves from the cocoon of grief.

And one day we do emerge - a beautiful butterfly - a stronger person, a more compassionate person, a more understanding person.

Be ever mindful that this, too, shall pass. We need to be ready for the cocoon to end. Are we going to be strong for those that are hurting?

God in his infinite wisdom has given us examples through his creation that we, too, are strengthening our wings to prepare us for whatever is to come.

God is in charge of our lives and we will go forward believing in his wisdom.

BARACK OBAMA

President of the United States of America

TO ALL TO WHOM THESE PRESENTS SHALL COME, GREETING:

BE IT KNOWN, THAT THIS DAY THE PRESIDENT HAS GRANTED UNTO

ALLEN EDWARD PERATT, SR.

A FULL AND UNCONDITIONAL PARDON

FOR HIS CONVICTION in the United States District Court for the District of South Dakota on an indictment (Docket No. 89-50074-02) charging violation of Sections 846 and 841(a)(1), Title 21, United States Code, for which he was sentenced on July twenty-third, 1990, as amended on May twenty-ninth, 1991, to thirty months' imprisonment and five years' supervised release.

THE PRESIDENT HAS DESIGNATED, directed and empowered the Pardon Attorney as his representative to sign this grant of executive clemency.

In accordance with these instructions and authority I have signed my name and caused the seal of the Department of Justice to be affixed hereto and affirm that this action is the act of the President being performed at his direction.

Done at the City of Washington, District of Columbia, on May 20, 2011

BY DIRECTION OF THE PRESIDENT

Ronald L. Rodgers

PARDON ATTORNEY

Presidential Pardon, 2011: After working multiple years to help others with recovery and re-entry, I applied for this Pardon. It took 14 1/2 years, but all the hard ministry work and patience resulted in receiving this honor.

El Cajon
Valley
High School
Graduation
1966

This photo was taken a few years after my release from the South Dakota State Prison system. Pictured are (back) our son AJ, Pastor Al, Teresa and Skylar.

Teresa and Skylar

AJ and his daughter, Deja Rose

(left to right) Teresa, Skylar, AJ, Pastor Al and Deja

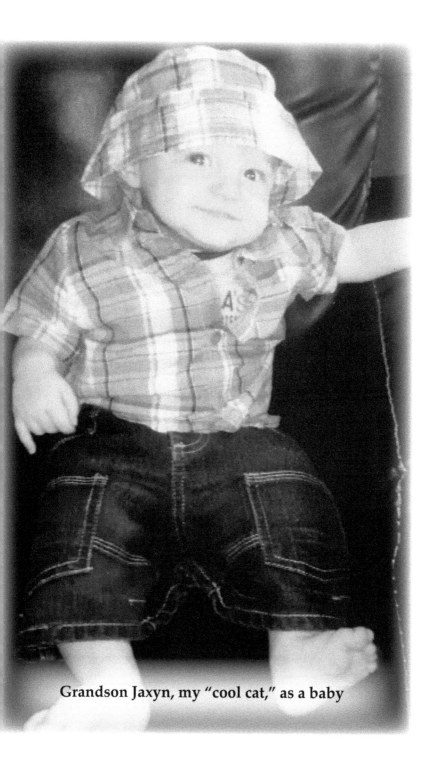

Grandson Jaxyn, my "cool cat," as a baby

Our wedding photo. (left to right) Bill Raishe (Teresa's Dad), Tom Peratt, Sr. (my Dad), Betty Peratt (my step-mother), Nasty Al, Teresa and a bridesmaid.

Set Free Security at Lifelight, largest Christian Festival in America at that time, the "Souled Out" stage that weekend.

Maximum Security facility where I served as Chaplain.

My "Church" clothes!

God is good, all the time!
With the Warden's approval, this was taken at the
South Dakota State Penitentiary maximum unit.

Riding a 2016 Suzuki Boulevard headed to Sturgis Tent
Revival at Sturgis Motorcycle Rally. Bearing the Set Free
"Servants for Christ" bike tank scripture, "If the Son
Sets you Free, ye shall be free indeed!" - John 8:36

Teresa and I at Falls Park (Sioux Falls) on a
1998 Moto Guzzi Italian bike. Many a Pow-Wow
held at the Falls over the centuries.

Teresa and I ministering with Set Free - On the Edge

Pastor Al on our Harley w/sidecar.
A 2019 flood swept away the bike and sidecar.

Pastor Al, Chaplain
Volunteers of America, Dakotas

Pastor Al and grandson, Jaxyn, "Papa's Riding Partner"

Pastor Al and Teresa at their workplace,
Volunteers of America, Dakotas.
Teresa ministered as a Chemical Dependency Counselor
while Pastor Al worked as a Chaplain.

Volunteers of America
A Ministry of Service

Ordained Minister

Al Peratt

has demonstrated exceptional knowledge of the holy scriptures of the Christian church and is thus rightly and canonically ordained. In granting this ordination, Volunteers of America entrusts this minister with the administration of the holy sacraments, and acknowledges this minister's belief in the Word of God and commitment to the ministry of service.

As I worked and ministered at different locations
- including jails, prisons, treament centers and hospitals -
I was required to present this
Ordination Badge.

Volunteers of America
A Ministry of Service

Al Peratt

FOR HIS FAITHFUL SERVICE AS NORTHEAST REGION REPRESENTATIVE
TO THE
CHURCH GOVERNING BOARD

CERTIFICATE PRESENTED
ON THE
SIXTEENTH DAY OF JUNE
IN THE YEAR OF OUR LORD
TWO THOUSAND THIRTEEN

LEO McFARLAND	MIKE KING
CHAIR	NATIONAL PRESIDENT & CEO
CHURCH GOVERNING BOARD	VOLUNTEERS OF AMERICA

**Recognition Certificate for service on
Volunteers of America Ministry Governing Board,
where I served until I was diagnosed with cancer.**

Certificate of Ordination

We, the undersigned, hereby certify that upon the recommendation and request of the ___Ridgecrest Baptist___ Church at ___Sioux Falls South Dakota___ which had full and sufficient opportunity for judging his gifts, and after satisfactory examination by us in regard to his Christian experience, call to the ministry, and views of Bible doctrine,

___Allen Peratt___

was solemnly and publicly set apart and ordained to the work of

THE GOSPEL MINISTRY

by authority and order

of the ___Ridgecrest Baptist___ Church at ___Sioux Falls South Dakota___ on the ___19th___ day of ___October___ 19 __97__

ORDAINING COUNCIL

Following my first Ordination, I became a Chaplain in the prison (1998). In addition, I was Music Director and Associate Pastor of Ridgecrest Baptist Church. After my second Ordination with Volunteers of America, I became Senior Pastor of Set Free South Dakota.

Presented To

Pastor Al

In Appreciation For Faithful
Ministry To His Brothers Behind
The Walls.

*"He put a new song in my mouth,
a song of praise to our God."
Psalm 40:3*

Prison Lighthouse Fellowship
October 2013

Recognition from a 2013 Prison Church Worship Service

PRESENTED TO

PASTOR AL PERATT

IN RECOGNITION FOR YOUR DEDICATED
SERVICE IN MINISTRY AT THE
SOUTH DAKOTA STATE PENITENTIARY

PRESENTED BY PRISON LIGHTHOUSE FELLOWSHIP

2004

Over the years, through 2019, when I retired due to
health concerns, I received recognition from numerous
Prison Church Worship Service Directors
such as those illustrated on these pages.

Pastor Al with his editor, Loretta Sorensen and
her husband, Alan, during the Sorensen's visit to
Volunteers of America, Dakotas Chaplain's office.

I can do all this through him who gives me strength."
- Phillipians 4:13

CHAPTER EIGHT

A NEW FAMILY:
OUR CHURCH

It was 1991 when I was released from South Dakota's Mike Durfee State Prison (MDSP). I had the usual "gate money" in my pocket: $50. I was also given a coupon worth $25 at the local thrift store. It would allow me to purchase some work clothes.

For a time, while I was in prison, Teresa was homeless. At the time of my release, she was receiving welfare benefits. She would lose them unless I was officially declared an ex-con living with my family on public assistance. To say that my journey on a new life path began at the "bottom" is an understatement.

Teresa expected my release to mean we would pick up with our lifestyle where we had left off. But I told her I wanted nothing to do with drugs or that drug lifestyle anymore. I had cut my hair, shaved my beard, and given up cursing. There were times when Teresa barely recognized who I was.

The apartment she had secured for her and the kids while I was incarcerated was two blocks from Ridgecrest Baptist Church in Sioux Falls. The pastor there had a short ponytail. Members of that congregation continually brought her food, clothing, and moral and spiritual support.

Since Teresa was raised in a home where her mother was a fifth-generation witch, she was suspicious of these "church people." What did they hope to gain in return for their kindness? She didn't attend their church or any other church while I was behind bars. Because of her godless background, she had a difficult time understanding that I had now surrendered my life to God.

I was very grateful to this church family who had watched over my wife and kids at a time when I could not. Not only did we begin attending the Friday night meals at the church, we were at Sunday morning and Sunday evening services every week. At first, Teresa and the kids were highly skeptical about my motivation for this new behavior. Nonetheless, I knew it was the direction my life must take.

Finally, as she watched me enjoy a new peace, Teresa was miserable enough to ask me what was causing me to be so at ease and so different.

I shared with her the plan of salvation:

1. Acknowledge God as the Creator of everything and accept our humble position in God's creation. "You are worthy, O Lord, to receive glory and honor and power; for You created all things, and by your will they exist and were created." (Revelation 4:11)

2. I am a sinner. "For all have sinned, and fall short of the glory of God." (Romans 3:23)

3. Because we are sinners, we are condemned to death. "For the wages of sin is death." (Romans 6:23) This includes eternal separation from God.

4. But God loved each of us so much that He gave His only begotten Son, Jesus, to bear our sin and die in our place. "God demonstrates His love toward us, in that, while we were still sinners, Christ died for us." (Romans 5:8) Although we cannot understand how, God says our sins were laid upon Jesus and He died in our place. Jesus became our substitute.

5. What must we do to be saved? "Believe on the Lord Jesus Christ, and you will be saved." (Acts 16:30-31)

6. It's evident in the Bible: believe in Jesus as the one who bore your sins, died in your place, was buried, and whom God resurrected. It's Christ's blood and resurrection that assures us of everlasting life when we call on Him as our Lord and Savior. "For whoever calls on the name of the LORD shall be saved." (Romans 10:13)

Are you ready to implement the plan of salvation by receiving God's gift of his Son, Jesus Christ? If so, believe in Christ, repent of your sins, and commit the rest of your life to Him as Lord.

It took some time and working through some ups and downs, but eventually Teresa also began working the 12-step program of recovery, taking the first steps on her new life path.

Together with our kids, we attended Ridgecrest Baptist Church. Initially, we committed to regular attendance. It wasn't long until I recognized a need within the church, and I wanted to do what I could to help meet it. During our time at that church, I served as music leader, then Associate Pastor, and later as Senior Pastor of Set Free Sioux Falls.

My first job was with a local communication company as office manager. My first paycheck was $155. That was gross pay. From that amount I gave the church a tithe of $15. Teresa threw a fit about the tithe. That initiated many "discussions" about why I gave 10% of my pay to the local church. But I was determined that I would focus on giving God thanks for this opportunity to take a different direction and being faithful to honor God in every area of our lives.

After attending the Friday night meals at church for several weeks, I inquired about being part of the team hosting the meals. The Senior Pastor assigned me the task of going from table to table, welcoming folks. However, I asked him if I could serve in a position with that group that no one else wanted. It was an effort to make my servant mentality a priority. My request was approved. I headed to the kitchen to take up the responsibility for washing pots and pans. I was elated to be serving God on the lowest rung of ministry during these first weeks and months of this new journey.

There were plenty of struggles between work, attending Alcoholics Anonymous and Narcotics Anonymous, taking time for family, and focusing on trusting God in every aspect of life. Little by little, day by day, God reshaped our hearts and minds, healed our emotions, and opened our eyes to truth. Only God could have strengthened us to humble ourselves and allow him to have his way in our lives.

It never occurred to us to seek any kind of limelight. Still, brothers and sisters in Christ could see the transformation taking place. They recognized our sincere desire to serve. Before long, our Senior Pastor approached me, placed the church key in my hand, and asked me to assist with church maintenance whenever possible.

It was one way that God affirmed the sincerity of our hearts and a means to confirm he was answering our prayers. We could trust him to open new opportunities as we grew and matured in the faith. I was happy to serve God and my Christian brothers and sisters in this way. I could never have imagined that it was just the first step of God's plan to give us greater opportunities for service in his kingdom.

My family and I attended Ridgecrest Baptist for about a year before the Pastor learned of my Seminary days at California Baptist College (currently California Baptist University at Riverside). At the time, the church's music leader had a debilitating condition that prevented him from raising his hands very high. The Pastor asked if I would lead hymnal songs during worship. I was happy to take that on every Sunday.

Before long, the church Choir Director approached me about taking over the choir. Man, where was this thing going? Here I was, an ex-con, leading music at church.

Well, it didn't stop there. Eventually, the Dakota Southern Baptist Director asked if I would lead an Association Choir for Christmas and Easter Cantatas. I was so humbled and ecstatic to serve God instead of drugs and alcohol.

During all these new opportunities, my family – who were getting on board with this new life direction – learned one of our church families didn't have food for the Thanksgiving holiday. We knew we had to respond.

We took our turkey over to this family's house. After they invited us inside, I took the liberty of opening a cupboard door. It was empty – no food! I told this single mother that my daughter and I would be back shortly. Through private, church, and fellow recovery peers, we raised enough money to go back to that family with 10 bags of food. They cried. We cried. Tears of joy!

That event was the beginning of a ministry we developed to help others during holidays. We called it "The Savior's Run!"

After two years of joyfully watching how God was now orchestrating the events of my life, I heard from the local sheriff of Minnehaha County Jail. Through his own church and local recovery networks, he had heard of me. He expressed his belief that I would be a likely candidate for coming into the jail and leading a Bible study "with language the inmates would understand."

Of course, I answered this call and began a simple Bible study, leading men through the book of Proverbs. It wasn't long before the transitional house across the street from the jail heard about what I was doing. Would I share Bible study at their home?

During all this time, my church was teaching so many biblical principles, which were familiar to me from my youth when my family attended Lakeside Southern Baptist Church. It didn't take much time to say, "You're already ministering to those whom others can't reach. Let's license you to preach the Gospel of Jesus Christ."

I want to emphasize that these leadership opportunities came to me as I kept a servant mindset at the forefront of each day. I didn't seek leadership roles or any kind of honor. This is a fundamental principle for all of us, ex-con or otherwise.

God calls us through the voice of leadership. Those opportunities acknowledge that our walk is now matching our talk. What a blessing!

The wall of my office at Volunteers of America, Dakotas is papered with certificates of achievement, and my license is the first one. I was licensed in 1993 and ordained in 1997. Wow, who would have ever thought?

It was in 1997 that the tower company I worked for folded in bankruptcy. For the next 15 years, I worked at Sioux Falls Hutchinson Technologies, Inc. After some eight years as an operator, I was promoted to Production Supervisor. At the same time, I was officially a bi-vocational pastor.

One of my first pastoral responsibilities was hearing Alcoholics Anonymous 5th Steps at a nearby treatment center, Keystone Treatment Center at Canton, South Dakota. I was invited to become part of this team after they heard my story during a Sunday evening presentation. I accepted their offer and have been a team member ever since. I'm still serving with them today. The folks at this treatment center are my brothers and sisters in different stages of recovery. I have 31 years of recovery myself.

Even after all these God-given blessings came into my life, he still wasn't done.

My bike riding days began in Riverside, California, when I was 17 and began riding a dirt bike. From there, I went on to ride many miles and many different motorcycles across America. The bike became a tool I could use to reach out with the Gospel to those who wouldn't usually grace the door of a church building. It also helped me connect with some who harbored past hurt or abuse that occurred in a church setting.

This ministry journey began with my wife Teresa and I attending the Sturgis Motorcycle Rally. We had both been there before. This time we weren't dealing dope. We were bringing the message of Jesus Christ in a very low-key manner.

At the time, we didn't ride for Christian Motorcycle Association (CMA). Instead, we had joined a Los Angeles ministry, Set Free. I rode Bedouin (commonly referred to as Nomad – alone) for them. It was just my wife and me.

After a few years, that small start led to the development of Servants for Christ, Set Free, Sioux Falls. Our Chapter began with six men, eventually growing to about 18 men. At the same time, my wife worked with the Chapter of Sisters In Service, an organization she founded. They developed their own patch. We were a relatively large group that visited jails, prisons, the local children's hospital, and many other venues.

Out of that group, we were led to open the first Set Free service at Ridgecrest Baptist Church. We had permission to meet on Saturday nights. The time frame worked well, since those of us lost in the darkness of alcohol, drugs, and criminal activity are often engaged in destructive pursuits on Saturday nights. Teresa and I were having a blast serving the Lord!

When our church service began bursting at the seams, we moved to a different site where Set Free – On The Edge was born. We held services from Saturday night through Monday, when our Serenity Group, Christian 12 Step, and women's group was held. Tuesday night, our Meth Anonymous group met; Wednesday night, we conducted Bible study, and Friday night was family night with movies and popcorn. On Sunday mornings, Teresa and I and our kids were often at local churches sharing the beauty of the changes

Jesus Christ was bringing about in these men and women.

At the peak of this ministry, we had Chapters in Sleepy Eye, Minnesota, and Beresford, South Dakota. There is now one in Sturgis, which was founded by Set Free Montana.

At this point in our lives, our children, AJ and Sky, were a mere 12 and 2 years old. AJ probably had the most difficult time adjusting to church. At our small Southern Baptist Church, Ridgecrest Baptist Church, AJ was at an age where he didn't fit in with the young children's church group and wasn't completely comfortable in the teenage church group. At that time, the teen church leader was a missionary who was still in college (she eventually married our fellow choir member). She was so good with AJ!

So, here comes AJ's Dad, like a gangbuster (no pun intended), and the family is just following. Two-year-old Sky reveled in church life. Many a Sunday afternoon our hands entwined as we walked to church to open the door for choir practice. At the time, I was blessed to lead the choir.

As practice started, Sky and I would turn on the microphones and sing our hearts out. We didn't know at the time that her singing was a miracle. Come to find out, she was partially deaf. Still, she could feel the rhythm of the music. Hearing the lyrics one time, she memorized the songs and sang on key all the time.

One summer, Teresa and I were blessed to travel with our church youth group on a mission trip to the inner city of Milwaukee. At the final meeting during that trip, I washed the feet of all the youth to show what Jesus did for his disciples.

These years brought incredible change to our family. Our children could have been in a 100% Outlaw Club if God hadn't changed my life while I was still in prison.

I didn't realize then that my years of ministry were just beginning. When my time at Hutchinson Technologies, Inc., came to a close, I began yet another ministry journey, serving at Volunteers of America, Dakotas.

Discussion Questions

1. Do you believe in God?
2. Why does Jesus' death on the cross matter?
3. Once you've committed your life to God, how does Jesus' death on the cross impact your daily life?
4. Do you believe he has a plan for your life?
5. Do you feel comfortable when you pray? If you pray?
6. Do you desire to learn to pray?
7. Have you prayed the prayer of salvation?
8. If you have prayed that prayer, what steps can you take now to deepen your relationship with God?
9. What steps can you take each day to follow his leading?
10. Consider reading Matthew 6:5-13 regarding God's instructions about praying.

If my people, who are called by my name, will humble themselves and pray and seek my face and turn from their wicked ways, then I will hear from heaven, and I will forgive their sin and will heal their land." – II Chronicles 7:14

CHAPTER NINE

GIVING GOD FIRST PLACE

One of the biggest challenges drug addicts face when released from prison is staying clean. I was no exception to that rule. I was glad that I had started practicing good habits before I was ever released from prison:

1. Get honest; stay honest. (the 10th Step)
2. Go to meetings, stay accountable. (3rd Step, 12th Step)
3. Do service work with a humble heart. Genuine humility is a crucial characteristic of those who turn their lives around. (12th Step)
4. Always remember that your actions create a reaction. Doing the right thing strengthens your commitment to right living. (Serenity Prayer)
5. Each day put one foot in front of the other. Some days are harder than others. But life does get better and doing what's right becomes more natural. (10th, 11th and 12th Steps)

Because of my new life, I was able to officiate at my Mom's funeral service. This is testimony to leading a clean and sober life. When I was immersed in a drug-addicted lifestyle, I probably wouldn't have even attended the funeral. I missed my brother's death in California when he passed away due to AIDS complications. Thankfully, in my clean and sober state, I was able to attend my father's funeral and the funerals of two other brothers. I was also able to officiate at a few family funerals.

My wife was skeptical from the beginning. She often told others, "I didn't believe him when he told me he had found God, that he was going to stay clean now. I was like, 'Okay.'"

She kept watching me and would later tell me she barely recognized me. Nasty Al was gone.

At one point, I told Teresa, "Honey, you used to be number one in my life. But not anymore. I have to put God first now. As long as I put God first, you will be in my life."

That was baffling to Teresa for a long time. It was so contrary to the relationship we had shared all our married life. Now she understands completely, and God is number one in her life, too.

The same day I was released from prison, members of our local NA fellowship picked me up to attend a meeting. They wouldn't allow me to say no. I continued to participate in meetings every day, after work. Sometimes it was hard to take that time away from family, away from things that I liked to do. But every time I went, I came home stronger. It was an invaluable part of my ongoing recovery.

I'll never forget the first time I was invited to speak at a treatment center. It was in 1993. My first reaction was, "No, you don't understand. I'm Nasty Al. You don't want me to talk to your fellowship."

That's one of the challenges ex-cons have to overcome. We sometimes struggle to believe we can change, that we have changed. That's part of the reason we have to keep attending meetings and church and keep working on our mindset. The more we do the right things, the more confidence we'll have in our ability to do what's right. The more we'll see our need to depend on God.

My parole officer assured me that, if I would willingly do what people were asking me to, I would get to the place I wanted to be: free and sober.

Something happens to us when we make an effort to help someone else. It makes you stop and take inventory: Am I doing what I'm telling others they need to do? Do I believe what I'm telling them they should believe? Reaching out to help someone else helps us see ourselves more clearly, helps bring our own walk of sobriety into sharper focus.

After I agreed to speak at Keystone Treatment Center (Canton, South Dakota), the Director, Carol Regier, asked me to commit to hearing some 5th steps at a treatment center.

The AA (Alcoholics Anonymous) 5th Step is an act of confession. In this step we admit to God, to ourselves, and to another human being the exact nature of our wrong. After voicing these things to another person, we write an inventory of those things we did wrong. It's critical to share this information as part of our recovery.

I told Carol that I didn't think I had anything to offer.

"All we're asking you to do is join our team, hear some 5th steps," she said. How could I turn her down?

I still wasn't convinced I could offer much to this woman's team or the people needing help. I agreed to an interview for this volunteer role. I prayed about it and asked God to show me how he wanted to use me. I was open to going in whatever direction he had planned.

I joined that staff and did all I could to help the people in that treatment center. At the same time, I was volunteering at Ridgecrest Baptist Church. I did janitorial work, helped serve food to the homeless in the church kitchen, and worked in the clothing room. As time went on, they asked me to help lead music and participate in their jail ministry. I made myself available at any time of the day to listen to people who needed to talk, those who were looking for counseling and mentors.

All these things led up to the time when our church approached me about becoming licensed to preach. It had been years since I first attended Seminary to become a worship leader. Now God had brought me down a long and winding road to reach out to others who, like me, lost their way in a dark and dangerous lifestyle.

At this point in my life, I had been out of prison for eight years. Through friends who had done prison time with me, I learned that prison authorities were asking snitches on the street if I was real. How thankful I am to say that they had to answer, "Yes." I was finally matching my walk to my talk. If you're going to talk the talk, you better walk the walk.

After my ordination in 1997, I answered my phone one day. I'd been around the Prison Warden long enough to recognize his voice. I immediately froze. Why was the Warden calling me?

"Hey," he said. "I want you to come in to visit with me. I have something I want to talk to you about."

"Why?"

"Don't worry," he told me. "You'll be able to go back home. Just come and see me."

The Warden asked me to start volunteering at the prison and begin speaking at some prison classes. His invitation took me by surprise. I wasn't sure I could meet his expectations. This seemed like a big step. After praying about it, I realized I had already been doing this kind of work for several years outside of the prison.

After investing some time in this role, I created a video about how to stay safe in prison. Authorities used it as part of orientation for new inmates coming to prison for the first time. In the video, I encouraged them to use their time in prison to do something constructive. I knew from personal experience that doing so would make them stronger and more ready to rebuild their lives once they were released.

Before I received the Warden's invitation to volunteer in this manner, the South Dakota State Penitentiary had never let a former inmate back behind the wall to be a Chaplain.

By 1997, I completed my studies and was ordained as a Southern Baptist minister. Now, as a licensed minister, I had the certification I needed to validate my work inside the prison. I surrendered myself to this new role. I have never looked back.

These experiences fully illustrate one of my favorite mantras: You don't need to seek leadership. Leadership will seek you when you match your walk to your talk.

Discussion Questions

1. In what way(s) has God recently blessed you?
2. Did he provide blessings to you when you were a youth? A young adult?
3. What blessings would you like to receive?
4. Do you desire both material and spiritual blessings? Why / why not?
5. Do you or are you willing to maintain a prayer journal?
6. What benefits do you believe a prayer journal would provide?
7. Has God led you to any role of helping others in your life?

*B*e strong and courageous. Do not be afraid or terrified because of them, for the Lord your God goes with you; he will never leave you nor forsake you." – Deuteronomy 31:6

CHAPTER TEN

LEARNING TO STAND

In mentoring and visiting with others who have done time, I have often heard comments about the painful road we face when deciding to change our lives.

There's no denying that I encountered my own challenges in walking that new path. When I was blessed with a new position at my job, I found myself in conflict with a former fellow inmate who also worked there. One morning, when I let him know I wasn't going to cover for his deliberate attempts to defraud our company, he came up over the desk. He made it perfectly clear he wasn't going to allow me to stand in his way.

At that moment, I had a choice to make. I could cave to the threat and collaborate in devious activities, or I could stand my ground and let them see I wouldn't be part of their criminal-thinking games. I stood my ground.

My friend, that's a tough place to walk. Anyone who's done time in prison is aware of the genuine threat our one-time peers can be. After all, peer pressure is a standard tool used to keep addicts and fellow criminals in line. When we live with intimidation and feel threatened, sometimes of our very lives, it helps ensure our loyalty to those who benefit by dominating us. We don't retaliate when they misuse us, and we don't snitch on them. We join them in illicit activities and become their surrogate.

Sometimes these kinds of challenges happen daily. If it isn't peers pressuring us to join them, it may be a fellow employee who has it in for us. It could be financial pressure that seems insurmountable. Or maybe we have an overwhelming sense of loss that we believe we can never overcome.

I had some bad days and didn't foresee promises of the many blessings that have come my way. I just trusted God to lead me one step at a time. My gratitude for what He did for me each day never wavered. At the end of a bad day, I gave him thanks. I wasn't in prison. My family was with me. I always had a job. We didn't dine on steaks and caviar, but we always had food. Our network of friends continually grew, and healing and restoration were happening with the entire family.

Three years after I was released from prison, in 1994, I had the opportunity to step into the role of Music Minister at our church. When I was approached about this opportunity, it was incredibly humbling. Twenty-eight years prior, I had entered seminary intending to complete a degree in music ministry. Now, I had the privilege of seeing God bring me through all the darkness and sin that had taken over my life for more than 20 years and restore the original plan he had for me.

It's hard to find words that really express the joy that opportunity brought. It was confirmation, from God, that I was doing what I set out to do. I maintained my focus on taking an entirely different path and allowed God to guide each step.

The joy of that moment and all the rewards it brought to my life for the years that followed made daily challenges seem less intimidating. While he didn't remove all the battles or remove all the pain that often came my way, God was true to His Word. He was with me.

After serving as Music Minister for a time, God opened another door. I was invited to serve as Associate Pastor at Ridgecrest Baptist Church. This blessing brought with it a new challenge. I recognized an opportunity to pick up where I had left off in 1966 when I turned away from God's call to attend Seminary. I committed to finishing the required Divinity courses to complete what I had started so many years ago.

In 1997, after more than two years of hard work, I was ordained as a Southern Baptist Minister. This opened even more doors for me in my prison ministry work of leading Bible studies. By this time,

I had heard more than 20,000 5th Steps (Alcoholics Anonymous 12 Step Program).

By the grace of God, in just a few years, I had moved away from the role of "Nasty Al," and I was now, "Pastor Al." Make no mistake, there were still people who were watching me, questioning whether I was "genuine."

This kind of scrutiny is another challenge ex-cons often face. It may come from family, bosses, co-workers, fellow church members, etc. When it happens, we have to set our minds on what we know: we are submitting our lives to God, and all the details are up to him. When we do what's right, there's no opportunity for anyone to "expose" misdeeds. Our actions won't bring us to a place where we don't belong, doing things that bring destruction.

Whenever this kind of confrontation occurred in my life, I did what God's Word instructs every Christian to do. "Therefore put on the full armor of God, so that when the day of evil comes, you may be able to stand your ground, and after you have done everything, to stand." – Ephesians 6:13

Discussion Questions

1. What challenges have you encountered as you took steps to change your life?
2. How have you overcome those challenges?
3. How do you define humility?
4. Do you aspire to be humble? More humble?
5. How can the example Jesus gives us help you become humble?
6. What did the humility of Jesus look like?
7. What steps can you take to serve others?

*T*hou wilt keep him in perfect peace, whose mind is stayed on thee: because he trusteth in thee." – Isaiah 26:3

CHAPTER ELEVEN

OUR GOD: AN AWESOME GOD

As God continued unfolding his plan for my life, I did my best to keep my eyes on him. I allowed him to lead and open doors to additional prison ministry opportunities, all in his way and time.

Despite some who doubted what God was doing in my life, God began opening more doors to ministry. In 1997, the same year that I was ordained, the Warden at South Dakota State Penitentiary asked me to come in and facilitate a group called "Impact of Crime on Victims." The group was intended to help inmates recognize who and how their crimes affected others.

At the time, it was unheard of for a former convict to come into the prison to assist with any prison activity. Again, a very humbling experience and further confirmation of God's desire to bless those of us who once turned our backs on him. Psalm 51:17 tells us: "My sacrifice, O God, is a broken spirit; a broken and contrite heart you, God, will not despise."

The following year, 1998, in light of my commitment to serving faithfully in the roles God had presented to me, a senior chaplain at the prison heard me share my testimony. It prompted him to invite me to join South Dakota's Chaplain Team. Then-Governor Bill Janklow signed a bill that allowed me to become the first-ever South Dakota ex-con to become a chaplain at the State Prison.

Our God is an awesome God!

In 2000, my wife and I had the opportunity to establish a church,

Set Free Ministries. It was designed to reach out to inmates and their families across South Dakota and the surrounding region. We wanted to minister to the "depressed, oppressed, addicted, and convicted." The ministry was a mission work of Ridgecrest Baptist Church. It was not the church your mama grew up with. Everything about it was biker oriented, including our dress, our music, our order of worship. We wanted bikers who were walking in spiritual darkness to feel comfortable in our services.

We held weekly worship services on Saturday evenings because that's when drugs and alcohol most dominate those who are addicted to them.

Using the "biker gang" experience and insight we acquired while immersed in the drug and alcohol culture, we reached out to those who still lived that kind of lifestyle. Other Christian bikers joined us to organize rides and meetings where we shared the Gospel and testimonies about how God changed our lives.

We helped homeless folks find temporary and permanent housing and connect with Christian brothers and sisters. They needed people who could stand beside them and mentor them as God changed their hearts, minds, and lives.

Many volunteers stepped up to help us. Each week we opened our doors to those lost in the blackness of addiction. We knew they were searching for something they sensed was missing from their lives. Through our church, we fed the hungry, counseled the broken, shared the truth of the Gospel, and welcomed all who came to our door.

Our approach to the ministry was in accordance with James 2:17 "In the same way, faith by itself, if it is not accompanied by action, is dead." We needed to exercise the faith God so freely gave us. We continually sought his leading regarding the needs of others. He was always faithful to provide guidance and the necessary resources.

During this time, I was still working at Hutchinson Technology. They gave me a job in 1992, and I remained there for 15 years. I also worked at Keystone Treatment Center in Sioux Falls from 1993 until 2009, when I retired from the position of Senior Spiritual Advisor.

In Matthew 25:39, God's Word tells us that, as Christians, we are called to minister to those in prison and those seeking to move out of the drug and alcohol scene.

"'When did we see you sick or in prison and go to visit you?' The King will reply, 'Truly I tell you, whatever you did for one of the least of these brothers and sisters of mine, you did for me.'"

God calls people like you and me, "brother and sister." Whether we are in the dregs of addiction or working to recover from all the wounds and losses, we need to know God loves us where we are. Some who don't know anything about us care about and love us, too.

The Apostle Paul was in prison. Before he recognized Jesus, he persecuted him, and oversaw the killing of those who called themselves Christians. No one knew more about God's love, about God's desire to rescue and bless us, than Paul.

Healing of our past rarely happens overnight. All people, regardless of their life experiences, must choose every day to seek Christ.

When I first began attending church and reading the Bible while in prison, I didn't get much out of it. But I kept going, kept listening. When we live in darkness for so long, repeatedly giving in to wrong compulsions, our hearts and minds are hardened to the truth. We lose our ability to trust others, to believe we can change and be a different person. If we don't have self-control in one area, it tends to spill over into other areas of our lives.

We must desire to change. It's a choice, one we have to make again and again. As we continue making choices to do what is right, the change occurs supernaturally. If we don't make up our minds to fully commit to change, we risk falling back into old habits, reaping the same consequences.

At one point in my life, I tried to debate with God and approach him from an intellectual standpoint. I was interested in making a "deal." But God doesn't make deals. He has a plan for our life that's designed to give us everything that's good.

In my early life, outside prison, I played the role of "Nasty Al." Always a tough guy, always dominating everyone and every situation. But when I was alone, or anytime I was forced to face what was going on inside me, I knew it was all a big game. I had to come to a point where I didn't want to play the game anymore.

God won't allow us to play games with him. Half-hearted

attempts to change will bring us right back where we started. We have to turn everything over to him.

Once we set out on a path of change, we shouldn't be surprised when doubts arise. Every Christian has experienced this. It's how Satan works to destroy us. In response to doubts, we turn to God, search His Word, and consider what he's done for us in the past. If he rescued us, delivered us from darkness, and blessed us with healing, we can trust he will complete what he began.

It's times like these when the encouragement and insight of a Christian brother or sister can help overcome the obstacle of doubt or worry. We need to stand with one another.

Being incarcerated is no excuse for delaying a commitment to change. If we can't change while we're in a structured, ordered environment, we don't want to. No matter where we are, there are obstacles to change. The obstacles themselves may be different, but they never go away.

The only thing that can stop us from changing is ourselves.

Discussion Questions

1. In what ways has Al's testimony helped you view church attendance?
2. Are you currently attending a church? Why/why not?
3. Do you feel comfortable in a church setting? Why/why not?
4. What is "church" about?
5. In what ways does serving others mirror what Jesus has done for us?
6. Do you feel drawn to serving others?
7. Have you envisioned ways you can be involved in serving others?
8. Do you believe God is calling you to serve in a specific type of ministry?

A new command I give you: Love one another. As I have loved you, so you must love one another." – John 13:34

CHAPTER TWELVE

LET HIS BLESSINGS FLOW

Securing work can often be a challenge for ex-cons. That's another reason we need to allow God to guide us through each day of sobriety and freedom.

In many different ways, I believe God immediately honored my commitment to turning my life around, blessing me before I was even released from prison.

Part of that blessing was a job as an office manager for C&B Towers, a company that is no longer in operation. In 1991, while I was a minimum-security inmate at the South Dakota State Penitentiary's West Farm Unit, I met the company owner through AA (Alcoholics Anonymous) meetings. I worked for them until they closed in 1993.

My next job was at Hutchinson Technologies, Inc. I began there in 1993 as a Production Operator, turning out the thin film assembly product that holds memory chips used in computers. At the time, 80% of the world's computers housed a small piece of metal like the ones I made. At that company, I became one of 12 Production Supervisors in the Sioux Falls plant. I credit that achievement to the Business Degree and Paralegal Degree I completed while I was incarcerated, and a lot of hard work.

It was 2009 when Hutchinson Technologies closed their doors and God opened the door for me to apply for a position in Sioux Falls with Volunteers of America, Dakotas (VOA), a non-profit organization. This was the second non-profit service opportunity for me. The first came as Associate Pastor for Ridgecrest Baptist

Church in Sioux Falls, South Dakota.

At the time, my wife, Teresa, already ministered at VOA/Dakotas as a Chemical Addiction Counselor. She was preparing to be commissioned as a minister. Part of her commissioning requirement was to read Susan Welty's "Look Up and Hope: The Life and Prison Ministry of Maud Ballington Booth." Maud was a co-founder of Volunteers for America (VOA), an advocate for prisoners and their families, and inauguration of the Volunteer Prison League.

Reading Maud's story helped me recognize that the church Teresa and I had developed, Set Free Ministries, and VOA were aligned in purpose and vision. Set Free Ministries ministered to the depressed, oppressed, addicted, and convicted. VOA (with 33 affiliates across the nation) is a faith-based human services organization dedicated to helping individuals and families in need. They also seek to create positive and lasting change through social services programs that empower those in need to live safe, healthy, and productive lives.

I learned that VOA/Dakotas was seeking a Community Service Specialist to work with juvenile offenders guilty of low-risk crimes. This was right up my alley. I applied for this position with the knowledge that our local VOA/Dakotas would be applying for a grant from their national office to support the development of a chaplain position at Sioux Falls.

In the first position, for 18 months, I presented classes to the juvenile offenders assigned to me. The course focused on how they could change their thinking to steer away from the troubled path they were traveling. Their parents had to attend with them.

Following the class, as the juveniles completed their commitment to the court, I assisted them in documenting their progress. That report was submitted to their Probation Officer.

When we say God moves in mysterious ways, this is definitely one of those examples. Who would have thought that a court system would ask an ex-inmate to serve as a guide and mentor for these adolescents? Only God knows!

Those 18 months were so gratifying as we held classes downtown in an old school building. The facility was donated by a local couple who purchased the building and gave it to the organization to serve homeless or poverty-stricken youth. It was called the

Bowden Center. By using this building, VOA, Dakotas offered several programs. Youth were able to use the gymnasium during the day. At night they were provided with a free meal.

So, picture this. I worked full time with VOA, Dakotas; part-time with Keystone Treatment Center, a recovery center; was full-time pastor at Set Free Ministries; and hosted Bible studies and Meth Anonymous Recovery meetings at church, with so many attending that the building overflowed.

All these things aligned perfectly with the prayers I had first prayed in prison. I asked our Heavenly Father to allow me to be the husband he intended I should be, and a father to my children. I prayed he would lead me to the right recovery meetings. I asked for some kind of service to pay back the damages I had racked up by leading others to sin and addiction.

God's patience, mercy, grace, favor – beyond our wildest dreams!

The VOA, Dakotas CEO/President suggested that, since my dream was to serve God in a big way, I should surrender to becoming a candidate for election to the VOA Church Governing Board. Few of the 33 affiliates of VOA sit on the National Ministry Board of Volunteers of America.

The suggestion drew me to spend much time in prayer about God's desire in the situation. I sought my wife's opinion as well as the input of my senior pastor, Rev. Jesse Moore, at Ridgecrest Baptist Church. Based on the results of those inquiries, I submitted my name. Now the wait for the vote to come in.

To my surprise, I was elected to serve a three-year term. Toward the end of the three years I had to step down from this opportunity to fight cancer. However, as part of this Governing Board, I served with some of the wisest, most caring people found across the United States. I participated in many Executive Leadership meetings held in cities such as Washington, D.C.; Alexandria, VA; Duke Divinity in Raleigh/Durham, North Carolina; Princeton Theological Seminary in New Jersey; Dallas; Simi Valley, California,; Chicago, etc. I thought to myself, "Really, Lord, why me?" I was experiencing so many blessings. From studies at Duke Divinity School to two Moral Injury Conferences at Princeton University. I was so blessed.

In 2016, my very own VOA, Dakotas CEO/President, Dennis Hoffman, led a nomination for the Leadership in Ministry award.

This honor was presented at the National Conference in Chicago, Illinois. The crowd's standing ovation brought tears of amazement and wonder at how powerful our God is. He wants us to know that he doesn't call us to him because we're qualified. He qualifies us to be called. What a testimony!

Through all these uplifting experiences, I continued as leader of Set Free Servants for Christ Motorcycle ministry. At the same time, Teresa was the leader of the Sister's In Service Auxiliary. Each group averaged about 15 members.

Some of our activities included gifting more than 150 Thanksgiving turkeys to congregants. For inmates spending the holiday in jail or prison, we brought the wives and children a tree, ornaments, lights, a ham with all the fixin's for a meal, toys for the children, and words of encouragement and support. We continued this ministry through the time our Set Free Ministries, Sioux Falls, was in operation.

Those involved with this project used our choppers, Asian bikes, Harleys, and anyone with a two-wheeled vehicle who wanted to help others in need. No more delivering meth – just God's love through his Son, Jesus Christ!

As of 2020, I am fully retired from all church or prison services. The only exception I make is occasional opportunities to assist with a weekend program by sharing a talk at the appointed time. It's important to me to continue sharing that, no matter our physical surroundings, we don't have to be locked up in our souls. We can be Set Free by the blood of our Lord and Savior, Jesus Christ.

My days are now occupied with two service roles. One as Chaplain at our affiliate Volunteers of America, Dakotas. The other is riding solo or Bedouin for Servants for Christ, a ministry headquartered in Great Falls Montana, led by the Reverend J.T. Coughlin. He allows me to ride in the Dakotas, serving others in need. I also serve as a part-time lecturer at Keystone Treatment Center, and spend many hours praying with others via a telephone prayer line I monitor daily in the Volunteers of America, Dakotas Chaplain's office.

Discussion Questions

1. How do you feel when others express appreciation for you and the work you do?
2. Do you believe God has abundant blessings for you throughout your life?
3. What steps can you/should you take in order to receive his blessings?
4. Does God ever withhold blessings from us because he's disappointed in us? Or do we miss blessings because we're not in a position to receive what he intends we should have?
5. Does God work in our lives even when we resist following his leading?
6. How does God make His sheep "lie down in green pastures?" (see Psalm 23)
7. How will you demonstrate to others the magnificence of God?
8. Why does God deliver the righteous?
9. Has God's deliverance always come in a way you hoped or expected?

*B*less the Lord, O my soul, and forget not all his benefits, who forgives all your iniquity, who heals all your diseases, who redeems your life from the pit, who crowns you with steadfast love and mercy." – Psalm 103:2-4

CHAPTER THIRTEEN

SELF-INFLICTED WOUNDS

As I look back on my life today, I recognize more and more signs of the addictive behavior that drove me for 40 years.

Early in life, I was hospitalized several times for abdominal hernias. I believe one instance was a rupture as the result of being a Little League catcher. I was hit with a baseball over and over. My coach finally put me in the right field, ending the painful experiences I had behind the plate.

The first Junior High School shower I took in front of all the other fellas stirred up a lot of comments, "Man, you sure are more mature than us – look at all his hair!" Little did they know that being shaved each time for those operations stimulated that hair growth.

But abdominal hernias weren't my only physical injuries. I also had issues with self-inflicted trauma. One symptom of my low self-esteem was the need for others to feel sorry for me. I wanted to be accepted, fit in. Being injured was one way to get attention, to be noticed.

Now I understand that, in the addiction world, it's common for us to feel like misfits. My own background includes being passed from one foster home to another, beaten with a belt, and molested. No wonder I wanted to inflict pain on myself.

My hostile approach to life led me to hang out in the tough part of my environment. There, it was no problem to find a reason to fight someone and display black eyes and bloody lips like a badge.

I soon learned that many girls loved a fighting man.

My young adult life was peppered with fights taking place on the wrong side of Los Angeles, getting shot, incurring wounds from a bullet that nearly took out my right testicle, and being run over by a truck, which meant healing in a full-body cast, then a partial body cast. By my own hand, my body was beaten up again and again. Not whining about it. I admit to putting myself in harm's way.

Those were the early-life injuries. Chronic obstructive pulmonary disease (COPD) came after 23 years of smoking cigarettes and so much pot I couldn't begin to calculate the amount. Smoking also included hashish, hashish oil, and – not crack – but smoking or basing cocaine. I spent eight years of my life addicted to these and caught a five-to-life prison sentence for smuggling a pound of heroin. For years I pushed my body to the limit. In the final years of addiction, before I was arrested and my world began to topple, I felt worthless, hopeless. I didn't understand there was therapy that could help me. It took going to prison to find the medical help I needed.

One reason I rejected help for my physical condition was the Criminal Creed: Don't Snitch. Don't tell anyone anything. Of course, it's excruciating to keep so much bottled inside.

It was after I went to prison that I was diagnosed with Hepatitis C. By then, the yellowing and even grey color of my skin were pretty apparent. At that point, lifers, who were already encouraging me in my recovery and Christian walk, recommended eating vegetables, fruit, and grains. I adopted a routine of exercise, running, lifting iron, and playing ball. When I wasn't exercising, I studied for my Business degree and Paralegal degree.

My next health challenge was type 2 diabetes, a condition that affects how your body metabolizes sugar. I had put on a lot of weight, shooting up to 279 pounds. Some of that was muscle; some was just plain old fat.

My greatest health challenge yet came in 2012. I had a swollen cheek and suddenly found myself unable to pronounce certain words when I was giving lectures at the Treatment Center. Pronunciation issues also occurred when I gave sermons at our Set Free Sioux Falls church and during prison services I regularly conducted.

I realized it was time to see a doctor. My wife Teresa, always my champion supporter, was by my side at the Veterans Administration (VA) clinic. When the doctor sat down to share his diagnosis, he didn't even have my chart in front of him. In a cold and emotionless manner, he proceeded to tell us just what needed to be done to cut out my tongue and voice box.

"Do you know what this man does for a living?" Teresa wasn't going to agree with the recommendation. "Have you even read his chart? What kind of doctor would come in and propose such news to a veteran without providing information about all the options?"

Needless to say, we quickly sought a second opinion. It was relieving to us to learn that, with 37 straight days of radiation followed by chemotherapy, we could be assured that there was a good possibility I would recover from this kind of tongue disease, squamous cell carcinoma. It was such a dangerous sounding condition.

Before we set out on this monumental journey, I thought kicking or withdrawing from heroin addiction was the hardest thing I would ever endure. Until then, we had no idea what a dark, dark world surrounds the process of removing cancer from the human body.

Initial radiation treatments didn't seem to sap my physical energy. But after a few weeks of daily radiation, the effects accumulated. I could no longer drive myself to treatment because I couldn't concentrate on driving. Very dear friends – Greg and Pam Sands – stepped up to serve as my guardian angels. Both of them – Pam, especially – drove me to appointments, then drove me home. Buck Hill, from the Dakota Baptist Convention and numerous others, also helped me keep appointments. I thank and bless you all!

Without a doubt, I can testify that cancer and other physical ailments can either bring you closer or drive you farther away from your Higher Power, who is my Lord Jesus Christ. The more entrenched we are in sin, the further we push away from God. The more sincere we are in seeking his will, the more these spiritual challenges lead us to prayer.

By the time my radiation and chemotherapy treatments were completed, I wasn't able to work. I was home every day. I was so exhausted from treatments that the smallest task caused me to feel I was swimming in mud.

Getting dressed took two or three hours. Just walking from one room to another required so much determination. I tried to cushion my family from realizing how weak and worn out I was so I could reduce their distress as much as possible. The experience was the toughest thing I have ever, ever gone through. Drug addiction, prison stays, recovering from injuries – even added all together those experiences don't begin to compare to the misery and pain of fighting Stage 4 cancer.

I won't even talk about treatments that were hindered by the VA. I and others witnessed delays that caused our illnesses to worsen as we waited 5 or 6 weeks for each appointment. My bride, the passionate advocate, even contacted Congressional representatives to see if they could assist in improving the care.

Following radiation/chemotherapy treatment, I made the first visit to my VA oncologist and collapsed in his office. From that point, I was in and out of a coma for 45 days. One night I died, and I would not have come back if it hadn't been for my wife, who alerted nursing staff, who then rushed to bring in the appropriate equipment necessary for my resuscitation.

Some have asked me if I saw Jesus during that experience. All I remember is a black vortex rushing me through what seemed like a dark tunnel. As suddenly as it had come on, it all reversed. Slowly, I awakened to what seemed like hell. It was a loud TV in a VA cancer ward. I remember thinking, "I didn't make it! Oh well, I gave it my best." I was sure it wasn't heaven!

For the next month, I was down in bed. When I was in a coma, I developed pneumonia, and doctors were afraid I would swallow wrong and aggravate my condition. I was fed through a machine-operated tube that went through my stomach wall and into my intestines. A port in my chest allowed nurses to retrieve blood since my veins were difficult to find due to past use of drug needles.

As of today, I've been cancer-free for nearly 7 years. However, no one is ever fully recovered from a cancer like this. Residual effects include a sinus condition requiring medication to slow the flow of mucus after my sinuses were destroyed by the treatment. My uvula – the teardrop-shaped piece of soft tissue in your throat that's made up of connective tissue, saliva-producing glands, and some muscle tissue – was destroyed. My eyes, my ears, and my teeth were never the best. Now I use a daily fluoride rinse to help protect my teeth, which are highly susceptible to decay.

Most recently, I'm dealing with destruction of my jaw due to radiation treatments. I'm undergoing numerous surgeries to remove decayed teeth - a result of chemotherapy. In addition to heavy rounds of antibiotics, I take daily hyperbaric oxygen therapy.

All that said, our choices as addicts have psychological consequences, too. We beat ourselves up so badly; some just commit suicide. Others live for a long time but suffer from the effects of their lifestyle. In my lectures, I often say, "Remember, every choice has a consequence."

Good choices, good consequences. Bad choices, bad consequences. Not judging, just saying.

If you're reading this and deciding to quit that alcohol/drug lifestyle, be sure to regularly visit your doctor for checkups as many health issues don't pop up until later in life.

If you have used heroin or methamphetamine, it's especially important to see your dentist for regular teeth cleanings. A conscientious dentist who understands your lifestyle will help you keep as many teeth as possible.

Discussion Questions

1. What physical consequences add to your struggle to change your life?
2. How do you feel about those consequences?
3. What are some psychological consequences of your past choices?
4. What resources has God given you to help when you question his loving, wise, and perfect sovereignty?
5. What are the benefits of resting in the sovereignty of God?
6. Why do some Christians struggle to be open and honest about experiencing trouble?
7. Why does God allow pain in our lives?
8. How has God used trouble in your life to change you and bring you to Himself?

Only fear the LORD, and serve him in truth with all your heart: for consider how great [things] he hath done for you." - 1 Samuel 12:24

"So then, my dear friends, stand firm and steady. Keep busy always in your work for the Lord, since you know that nothing you do in the Lord's service is ever useless." – 1 Corinthians 15:58

CHAPTER FOURTEEN

MAKING HIM LORD OF ALL

I want to close my book with words of encouragement for all who read it. Regardless of the point in our lives that we begin to serve God, it takes a lot of work. Each day, each hour we must persevere, believing in Jesus Christ as not just Savior, but Lord.

In the years following my decision to allow God to guide what was left of my life, I worked in a wide variety of ministries. I've served in Veteran's programs, numerous volunteer programs, worked at local thrift stores and taken on the role of Prison Team Leader.

In 2000, God gave me a vision for our Set Free Ministries, a biker-oriented church designed to serve the depressed, oppressed, addicted and convicted. Our dress, music and every aspect of the ministry reflected the biker culture.

As of 2020, I retired from the full time position of Set Free Senior Pastor. I also retired from South Dakota State Prison scheduled worship services and reduced my hours at the Keystone Treatment Center to part-time.

God has rewarded my faithfulness to him in so many ways. A few of these include:

1990/1999: Commuted sentence of Life to 75 years, released from parole 14 years early

2005: I received the South Dakota Department of Corrections Employee of the Year Award

2009: Began working at Volunteers of America/Dakotas,

receiving the National VOA Chaplain's Grant in 2010.

2011: President Barack Obama presented me with a Presidential Pardon, completely wiping out my prison record

2012: Fought cancer and now in remission

2014: Sioux Falls Mayor Proclaims April 6, 2014 as Pastor Al Day

2016: Presented with Volunteers of America Leadership in Ministry Award at their Annual Conference in Chicago, IL

2013-2019: Helping the Less Fortunate With a "Hand up, not a Handout."

When I was caught up in the drug and alcohol scene, trying to prove how great and invincible I was, I could not have imagined all the blessings God was holding for me. He was just waiting for my eyes to be opened and my heart to turn from all the destructive thoughts and habits that dominated my life.

So, how does all this relate to you and your life? Are you familiar with John 3:16? It says, "For God so loved the world that he gave his only begotten son, so that whoever believes in him shall not perish but have everlasting life." God wants you, me, and every person he ever created to spend eternity with Him. But it's our choice.

We cannot walk in God's peace or receive the blessings he has planned for us if we insist on going our own way. If we decide to trust him, obey and follow him, he will build up our faith, encourage our heart, pour out joy and peace in every part of our life.

Just like me, you have to make a decision. Are you willing to put God in the driver's seat? Will you trust him to bring you through all the challenges you experience in life?

My prayer for you is that you don't turn away from answering these questions. I pray you let go of all the darkness and empty promises that you hold on to when you choose to live without God and his guidance.

When it was my time to choose, I found that I was not alone. God was with me every step of the way. He had so much more for me than I could have asked for. He'll be there for you, too.

Whenever we recognize sin in our lives, we need to confess it and receive God's forgiveness. That's our first step to living a life of honesty. "For if we confess our sins, he is faithful and just to forgive our sins and cleanse us from all unrighteousness." – 1 John 1:9

If you're ready to take a new path, pray the following prayer and then find fellow Christians who can support, mentor and help you grow in the faith.

"Lord, I am grieved and humbled to recognize the sin in my life. I confess that I have sinned, and I am putting my faith in you and your Word to heal and restore all I have lost. I gratefully receive your gift of salvation. I am ready to trust you both as Savior and Lord. Thank you for bearing my sins and giving me the gift of life. Come into my heart, Lord Jesus. Be my Savior and my Lord. Amen."

You are welcome to use the scripture featured in each chapter and the questions at the close of each chapter in a small group setting, in your home, church or during break time at your work environment. Both the scriptures and questions are intended to help readers dig deeply into their own lives to find healing and the strength to follow a new path.

My contact information:
Restoration Baptist Church, 1034 N. Spring Avenue, Sioux Falls, SD, 57104
Or
Volunteers of America, Dakotas, 1401 W 51st St, Sioux Falls, SD 57105.
pastoral.peratt@gmail.com